Wort & Worms Washbacks

John McDougall & Gavin D. Smith

Wort Worms & Washbacks

MEMOIRS FROM THE STILLHOUSE

ANGELS' SHARE

Wort &
Worms &
Washbacks

The Angels' Share is an imprint of
Neil Wilson Publishing Ltd
303a The Pentagon Centre
36 Washington Street
GLASGOW
G3 8AZ
Tel: 0141-221-1117
Fax: 0141-221-5363
E-mail: info@nwp.sol.co.uk
*http://*www.nwp.co.uk/

First published in October 1999
Reprinted June 2000
Text © John McDougall & Gavin D. Smith, 2000
Illustrations © James Hutcheson

A catalogue record for this book is
available from the British Library.

ISBN 1-897784-65-1

Typeset in Bembo and Alleycat
Designed by Mark Blackadder
Printed by WS Bookwell, Finland 2000

Contents

Abbreviations

ABV	Alcohol by volume
CE	Chief Executive
DCL	Distillers Company Ltd
EGM	Extraordinary General Meeting
GMD	General Manager of Distilleries
gpb	gallons per bushel
HMC&E	Her Majesty's Customs & Excise
J & B	Justerini & Brooks
lpa	litres per annum
MD	Managing Director
MDA	Malt Distillers Association
MW	Master of Wine
ppm	parts per million
QAM	Quality Assurance Manager
RPB	River Purification Board
SMD	Scottish Malt Distillers
SWA	Scotch Whisky Association
UD	United Distillers
UDV	United Distillers & Vintners
UO	Unattached Officer

Reviews of Wort, Worms & Washbacks

'A grand full-bodied read. Cheers!'

Ian Smith, *The Scots Magazine*

'... full of humour and interest.'

The Highland News Group

'... an excellent purchase whether you have any interest in whisky or not ...'

The Ileach

'These behind-the-scenes tales of not-so-everyday life in the whisky industry will have you reading and re-reading and ... reaching for a drop of the article.'

Dundee Evening Telegraph & Post

'... a very human, and at times very funny account of life within the world of whisky-making ... a very different whisky book, and one which should keep you engrossed from start to finish. I am told that it is already required reading within the whisky industry and that a number of old-timers with tales to tell are kicking themselves for not getting in there first. I doubt if they could have done a better job.'

Tarbert Campbell, *Perthshire Comment*

Chapter 1
Speyside:
Early Days at Aultmore

Looking back, I suppose the staff at Aultmore must have wondered what sort of a playboy they had got for their new trainee manager when I drove up to the remote, old-fashioned Speyside distillery one dreich December day in 1963 in my Mark I 2.4 litre Jaguar. Their doubts, I was later to realise, must have been compounded by the fact that the distillery manager chose nothing more ostentatious than a push-bike as his personal mode of transport.

The Jag was a legacy of working in my father's grain company in Edinburgh. He had been paying me the comparatively generous sum of £750 a year, and I had lived at home, making only modest contributions to my keep. Given those circumstances, the car was a reasonable indulgence. When I joined Scottish Malt Distillers – the malt whisky-making division of the great Distillers Company Ltd – in 1963, aged 22, my annual salary fell to £500, out of which I had to find £6 per week to pay for my digs at Aultmore. Also, being a young man and a rugby player, there was beer to buy. The Jaguar had a greater thirst than I, and ultimately was to become an unreasonable extravagance, even in those days of comparatively cheap petrol. Its replacement was a Volkswagen Beetle! If my father had paid generously, he expected hard work in return, and I was certainly no playboy. I was physically very fit, and more than capable of getting my hands dirty, which was just as well, considering some of the jobs that lay ahead of me at Aultmore.

My father and I got on well on a personal basis, but we found it difficult to work together because he was so entrenched in his ways and wasn't prepared to move the business forward in what I thought was the right way in a changing climate. He was approached a couple of times to sell the company to firms that were getting bigger, but he carried on. Personally, I thought it would have been better if he had sold out and got an equity stake in a larger company; it would certainly have suited me better! As he got older and I got on in the whisky business, he accepted that I had made the right career move.

After parting company with my father, I approached John Waugh, director of the DCL cereals division, who suggested that the best career opportunities in the company for a young man at that time probably lay in the production side, where my knowledge of cereals would still be of real use, as many distilleries continued to do their own malting. The scientific laboratories that distillers have at their disposal nowadays just didn't exist then – it was all about practical evaluation. What I learnt about barley with my father was exceptionally valuable. As far back as 1948 I used to go around farms with him when he was buying and selling barley. I had the idea that the whole world revolved around the stuff! One of the differences between my distillery training and that of someone in a similar position today is that while they know the theory, they haven't had the practice that I had, because with centralised maltings there is now no need for it.

I was taken on by DCL as one of 12 management trainees, and the training programme at that time was very forward-looking. It was a period when the company was trying to move away from the idea of the distillery manager as a cloth-capped, boiler-suited foreman figure into a more professional management figure, so they recruited people from various backgrounds, such as accountancy, agriculture, and engineering, and each one was allocated to a distillery within the group. I was sent to Aultmore, which was situated off the Buckie road, some three miles outside the town of Keith, quite high up and isolated.

This was a time of what seemed like a never-ending boom as far as Scotch whisky sales were concerned, and everyone in the industry was looking towards a tremendously buoyant future. DCL was rebuilding lots of its distilleries, and developing existing plants. For example, at Glenlossie they built on a new section and called that Mannochmore while at Glendullan they eventually had Glendullan Number One and Glendullan Number Two. These were all distilleries in their own right, and so the trainees they were taking on were the managers of the future for these units as well as the existing ones.

Speyside then, as now, was the heartland of whisky-making, though in the sixties there were still many family companies which have since been absorbed by the multi-nationals. In Rothes, on the Spey, a town which is nearly all distilleries, Glen Grant was privately owned, as was Longmorn, and Benriach, although not working at the time, was also still in private hands. There were certainly a lot more Scottish-owned and run distilleries than there are today. Eventually DCL was to be absorbed by Guinness during the eighties and in 1998 a merger with chief rivals Grand Metropolitan led to the creation of Diageo, the biggest spirits company in the world.

Elgin is the 'capital' of Speyside, and remains very much a whisky town – the place is steeped in distilling lore. I remember a television programme on a Sunday night being broadcast from Elgin during my time at Aultmore. The Revd Henderson was the minister, and he took some criticism from the straight-laced people in the church when he actually put up a prayer for 'The Dram'. What he meant, of course, was that he was praying for all his parishioners who worked in the distilleries surrounding Elgin. It wasn't just about making whisky, not simply an industry, it was a way of life.

Our practical training with DCL was very comprehensive, especially at Aultmore, which was the most old-fashioned distillery belonging to the company. It was so old-fashioned that you learnt everything about how to make whisky in the most basic way imaginable. There was also theoretical training to complete, and we were sent tomes and tomes of information, written by DCL's experts on barley, malting, energy conservation, effluent disposal, coopering, warehousing, and even the right coal to use for the boilers. Every three or four months we were taken away for a couple of days and given lectures by these specialists, who were all university graduates, the boffins of the DCL group. That training course was, in effect, the forerunner of the brewing and distilling degree course now run at Heriot-Watt University in Edinburgh.

It was tremendous training, and very character-building, because a lot of the young men who had come into the business did not have rural backgrounds. I was slightly fortunate in that although I'd been educated in Edinburgh, I was really a country boy. I'd never lived in the city until my father moved his operation to Edinburgh in the mid-fifties. I was born in Kirkcaldy in Fife, and really enjoyed the life of a country lad outside of school, so it was not too difficult for me to adapt to country life again, and it was something I actively wanted to do. In earlier years I had fancied being a farmer, and I felt that distilling was the next best thing.

For the boys from cities, going to a place like Aultmore was akin to putting somebody on the moon. Some of them found it very difficult to adjust. One of the things that kept them sane, I think, was a love of sport. They had nearly all gone to rugby-playing schools, just as I had, and a lot of us actually met for the first time at the Moray Rugby Club in Elgin.

The Customs & Excise service also had its trainees, who were known as UO's – Unattached Officers – and they were moved around the distilleries too, so we had quite a rapport with them. They were young men like us, and they helped us build up a network throughout the industry; that way we got to know people from other companies, because very often we were introduced to them by the excise trainees.

The UO's used to meet up with the distillery trainees three or four times a week – they loved a good party as much as we did – and we would rendezvous in various establishments the length and breadth of Speyside. Sometimes the sessions wouldn't end until three or four in the morning, then we would all jump into our cars and drive home – this was well before the coming of the breathalyser! Inevitably, next morning, the excise trainees would turn up late for work, whereas we had to be there at eight o'clock as usual. We frequently had to wait for the spirit charge to be taken because they couldn't get out of their beds. They would arrive to find a distillery manager pacing up and down, furious because his filling of spirit was being held up, and so in turn the warehousing. When the UO did turn up, his excuse would be something like, 'John McDougall kept me up drinking till four in the morning.' The manager would respond, 'Well, despite that, he was here on time, and you weren't.'

The UO's were great lads, but most of them didn't get the careers they thought they would have, being attached to individual distilleries, because in 1967 the Government undertook a Spirit Review, which was the beginning of the phasing out of resident excise officers at each distillery. By the early to mid seventies, officers in distilleries were fast becoming a thing of the past. Prior to that, one officer per distillery was the name of the game, and it was up to the distillery to provide a house on the premises for the officer to live in. After that, one officer was responsible for three or four distilleries in his area, and that was eventually phased out completely. Distillers are now self-policing and so there are no new trainees taken any more.

The UO's played rugby with us as well, and we knocked hell out of each other during training matches. If it was a young officer you were tackling, you might go in a bit harder, because it was one of the few ways you could get your own back! Another way was to get them totally paralytic while you were still on your feet and comparatively sober. As the majority of them were English, we used to rib them mercilessly about their inability to take their drink.

Those of the DCL trainees who had graduated to be assistant managers at particular distilleries were usually allocated houses, and sometimes we would meet up at someone's house for a drink or two. Or more. I remember one occasion at the assistant's house at Craigellachie Distillery when a party started on Thursday evening, resumed on Friday night, and then carried on again after those of us who had to work Saturday morning had finished for the weekend. It just kept going and was followed by a mysterious outbreak of 'flu' which kept people in their beds until Tuesday or Wednesday. It was all fuelled by duty-free samples and spirit acquired by the excise officers – supposedly for testing their instruments.

The positive side of all this integration between 'them and us' was that we developed an understanding of each other and our respective positions, and it made for very positive working relationships. It was actually good for the industry. There was a common bond, and the officers became very protective of their allocated distilleries, and took a real pride in them. They would compare notes and boast about how the distilleries in their group were more efficient than others.

After rugby matches in Elgin we would often gather in The Thunderton in Thunderton Lane, which was run by Bert Lascelles and his wife. Bert had been in the Colonial Service and he lived as though he was still in it, always wearing a kilt. The Thunderton was very popular, principally because it boasted the most beautiful barmaid in Morayshire – an absolutely gorgeous creature by the name of Edna. It was every young man's dream to get close to Edna, but she kept herself very much at the other side of the counter, though she did finally succumb to the charms of a young UO – thinking, probably wisely, that he was a better bet than a would-be distillery manager. We would usually have had about ten pints by the time we arrived at the Thunderton around eight o'clock, and during the course of the evening we'd have a fair few more. When we got to the stage of inebriation where Bert would take our car keys from us to prevent us driving anywhere, Edna would say, 'Is it time for the Revolving Room, lads?' and would deposit six of us into one spare bedroom. They were happy enough to do this, because they knew we would be paying for breakfast in the morning. It was called the Revolving Room because on one famous occasion, a great friend of mine, Ricky Robertson, got up in the middle of the night, and as he passed it, the wardrobe door swung open and hit him in the face. He turned around, only for it to hit him in the face again as it swung shut.

The old Customs & Excise service was sometimes criticised unmercifully by the industry, but there was a discipline there, you had to comply with the regulations. The whole industry was obliged to operate within that framework of rules, no matter which company you worked for. You always knew what the Inland Revenue regulations were, and it is much more difficult today. Nowadays you have self-regulation, and each company has its own attitude towards that. The directors of most of the whisky companies were from similar backgrounds to the Customs & Excise officers, and had the same approach to their jobs. An awful lot of them had seen military service, and they took the Ministry of Defence attitude to life back with them into the whisky industry. For me, being in such a strictly controlled environment was a real eye-opener. You were dealing directly with what the Government and the industry recognised to be 'revenue'.

One of the great influences in my training was the manager of Aultmore distillery, who was very much a gentleman of what you might call the 'old school'. John Nicol had been born and brought up at Balmenach Distillery, so he had been in distilling literally all his life, and had seen the business develop from before the First World War. He was a very upright person in all senses. He stood well over six feet tall, always wore a check cloth cap and immaculate tweeds for work. He brought with him a very Victorian attitude to life in general. He was married but had no family of his own, and he found it very difficult to understand why young men like me could conceivably need time off on a Saturday afternoon to go and play rugby when I could be shovelling coal in from a railway wagon and topping up the coal bays for the stillhouse. He had to accept, however, that things were changing, though he was also a gentleman who didn't believe in motor cars; he thought they were for lazy people. If you needed to go anywhere beyond cycling distance you took what he called the 'autobus'.

●   ●   ●

Like many distilleries at the time, and indeed long after, Aultmore was always short of water in summer, despite the fact that its name is Gaelic for 'big burn'. Lack of water was the reason for a long closed or 'silent' season when the distillery did not make whisky. There wasn't sufficient water for cooling, and also you couldn't make good whisky if the water wasn't cool enough because the spirit would run too hot and be rough. So the manager was always looking for water for Aultmore from about April onwards each year, and we used to close the place around the end of May anyway. It stayed silent for at least three months. Nicol would frequently set off on his bicycle up to the water supply to check on the situation, and so he was known by all the workforce as 'Chasewater Charlie'.

He was exceptionally keen that his trainees did well as he did not want to be seen as a failure in any shape or form, and I was reminded from day one that none of the trainees at Aultmore had ever failed the distillery examination set by the company, and he did not wish me to be the first, as it would reflect badly on him. He only had two years to work until he retired, and there was no way he was going to go out as a failure on account of somebody else.

In those days, the basic working week was 48 hours, and we had to work on a Saturday morning irrespective of anything else. Sometimes, however, because of the nature of the whisky-making process, we had to go in on Saturday afternoons as well. Some trainees with less strict managers were allowed time off to play rugby anyway, which irked me, and I was warned that if I ever got injured playing rugby and couldn't turn up for work there would be hell to pay. On one occasion I dislocated my shoulder and I didn't dare tell anyone I had done it. I went to work regardless, and at that stage I was shovelling coal to fire the stills!

As I got to know the men I worked with, they would offer to cover Saturday afternoon shifts on an unofficial basis to allow me the chance to play rugby. In return, I would work a nightshift for them if they wanted to go to a dance. You wouldn't have thought it could be so difficult to get a game of rugby, but a number of factors tended to conspire against me. One Saturday lunchtime I was about to make a surreptitious exit from the distillery in order to play in Elgin when Charlie peered around his office door and asked me where I was going. As I was carrying a pair of studded boots at the time, there seemed little chance of getting away with any sort of untruth. 'I'm away to play rugby, Mr Nicol,' I responded, as casually as I could. 'Andrew Mitchell is covering my shift for me.' 'Is he?', replied Charlie, with a very austere look about him. 'Well I don't know. I need to be asked about arrangements of this sort. It just will not do.' With that, his head popped back into his office, and as I hadn't actually been told not to go, I made a quick escape, before he could reappear and insist I spend my afternoon attending to fermentation rather than risking life and limb on a rugby pitch.

The weather could cause problems with regard to rugby as Elgin was about 20 miles from Keith, which was quite high up, while Elgin was in the low ground. I could be in Keith on a Saturday morning in winter with a foot of snow around me, imagining the game couldn't possibly be played, only to be phoned and told it was a beautiful day in Elgin and that I was playing in the afternoon. There was no guarantee the Jag and me would be able to get home again that night. In 1964 I was elected captain of Moray Rugby Club, but before I could accept the captaincy I had the unenviable task of asking Charlie for permission. 'Let me consider the matter,' he replied gravely, and a couple of days later gave his consent.

The delicate state of my finances also played its part in my sporting life. One Saturday I was to captain the team in a match at Aberdeen, but there was barely enough petrol in the Jag to get me from Aultmore into Keith, never mind as far as Aberdeen. My salary was due to be paid on Monday, but in the meantime, my account was empty and all I had in my pocket was a bit of loose change. I had a very old-fashioned Bank of Scotland manager named Charlie Reidford, and I approached him for a temporary overdraft to the tune of five pounds. 'Well I don't know about this at all,' he said, peering at me over half-moon specs, 'It means you'll be in debt. It's five pounds less you'll have in your account on Monday, you know.' Eventually a compromise was reached, and he gave me four pounds.

●　　●　　●

When I was there, Aultmore was very much a distilling community. It had a spur railway line in those days, off the Strathspey line from Keith and the main Inverness-Aberdeen line. All of the materials for the distillery were delivered by train, and the spirit which was not being warehoused on the premises went out by rail. At that time there was a staff of 22, whereas today's modernised Aultmore has about six or seven. I would call it a unit now, not a distillery really. They don't fill spirit into casks at all, and there is not a cask on the premises. Everything is taken away by road tanker.

There used to be 12 distillery cottages, each occupied by what were deemed to be key staff, the people who could be called out at a moment's notice should there be a problem. The rest of the staff were drawn from the area round about – a few from Keith itself, and others from little crofts, which they worked as well as having jobs in the distillery. Distilling has its roots, of course, around farms, which traditionally had farmworkers' or cottar houses, and this community was a parallel to that. I used to be invited by the men during the odd hours we had off to go into Keith for a pint, which often ended up as far too many pints. In a way this was a very good part of my training, because it allowed me to get inside the minds of the staff who, at that time, were actually the people who operated the distillery. This was rather frowned upon by Chasewater Charlie, who thought I should get to know the men, but not that well!

I had to be able to gain their trust, however, so that they would teach me how to make whisky. The manager was not in the distillery all the time, and he certainly wasn't bringing down mashes and showing you how to mash and how to drain and all the rest of it. I had to gain the men's trust and they had to gain mine. I then learnt some of the shortcuts, some of the bad habits. It was vital for me to be able to understand the psyche of people who were probably going to be doing those jobs until they retired. That was their life, they weren't going anywhere else, but I was, provided I passed my exams. Whisky-making and its mystique might look very romantic to the outsider, but at the heart of it, especially in those days, was a group of people doing fairly repetitive and mundane jobs.

I lodged in one of the distillery cottages with the Stronach family, and Nellie Stronach, my landlady, came from Portsoy on the coast. Many of the little fishing villages were getting quieter than they had been in the past, and quite a few of the fisherfolk were migrating from the coast to look for other jobs. Nellie had come inland and married Robbie Stronach, who worked at Aultmore. Nellie introduced me to boiled beef and carrots, made into a kind of soup, which became something of a staple diet. I got this four times a week, with fish once, and a special treat of tatties, liver and onions, twice a week. Returning from a hard day at work, my appetite would sometimes flag at the thought of the predictable meal ahead of me. One evening, I was due the liver and onions 'treat', which at least did something to sharpen my hunger, only to be greeted by the momentous news from Nellie that she had made me 'something for a wee change' for dinner. My imagination and my appetite soared in equal proportions. A pork chop perhaps, maybe even a pie. I sat at the table with happy anticipation as Nellie bustled through from the kitchen and set a plate down in front of me. 'It's your favourite', she said fondly, 'only a bit special.' It was boiled beef and carrots, but with some peas mixed in. I tried to smile gratefully, and picked up my knife and fork.

Nellie was actually a very kind lady who became something of a mother figure to me. Her daughter had married a man called Peter Lochrie who also worked in the distillery, and they lived just a couple of doors away. It was that kind of very close-knit society. I found it quite flattering that eventually I became part of their community, and if things went wrong for me there were people who cared and could help. That was something I never expected to achieve when I went there, so when I did eventually leave Aultmore, I was very sorry to go. In a way I feel that young men coming into management in the industry today are at a disadvantage, because inevitably they are still going to be sent to what may be termed 'outposts', yet without having experienced the practical way of living in such communities it is very difficult for them to go in and make an assessment of people they probably don't really understand.

One of the features of distillery life in those days was the practice of 'dramming'. Usually this consisted of giving the workers at least two drams per shift, and some distilleries were very generous and dished out three. Many plants would use the new spirit, called clearic, and the whole process was something of a ritual. Aultmore's brewer was Sandy Burgess, and he was known as 'Sandy Aye Mun' because that was the expression he used most frequently. Sandy would go round and make it known to everyone that it was dram time, and they would all go down to his office at the end of the stillhouse and stand in a straight line while he dispensed the measures, on which, of course, no duty had been paid. This was spirit at about 63%ABV, or the old 'eleven over proof', as it had been reduced in the filling store down to that strength. The theory was that this gave the men an incentive to work hard for another four hours, when the next dram would be dispensed. It was such a ritual that people developed their own style of taking the dram. One of the tunroom men, Jimmy Marshall, would just raise his arm and throw it back, and on one occasion the brewer decided to pour him a measure of water. Jimmy took it in his usual manner, and he was half way back up the stillhouse before he suddenly stopped, turned with a face that looked as though he had just bitten into a lemon, and said, 'You rotten bugger, that was water!'

Not all drinking that went on in the distillery was done with the approval or knowledge of the management, however. At Aultmore the head maltman used to disappear with a five-gallon measure into the tun room where the washbacks were. He would then get some of the wort which was being pumped from the mash tun up to the washbacks, add a little yeast from the yeast tank and make a sort of beer which would be drinkable after two or three days. I only tried it once, and it was awful stuff. It was known locally as 'The Besom Jean', though I never quite understood why. All I can imagine is that someone called Jean who was a 'besom' possibly made the first lot. 'Beel' Clark was known to take the odd sample from the washbacks and drink it. For some reason the wash was known as the 'Joe'. I can only think that 'Joe' was the first man caught drinking the stuff. This sort of practice was quite widespread. Any manager who really knew his distillery and his workforce would probably be aware of what was going on, but a blind eye would be turned, provided the men weren't falling about drunk all over the yard.

The first New Year I was at Aultmore we worked on New Year's Day, just as on Christmas Day. I was detailed to clean the plant after celebrating Hogmanay all night, getting drunk with my new-found friends, the distillery men. We had to report at 6am and most of my colleagues were pretty paralytic. I don't think I was too sober myself. We were confronted by the teetotal Charlie, along with Sandy Burgess, who was effectively the foreman, and they wished us a Happy New Year before dispensing generous measures of clearic. This was to encourage us to work well as we had to enter the wash still in order to scour or 'scoor' it clean of burnt-on yeasty solids. Having been given the *clearic* we were then accused of being drunk on duty and unfit to work!

One small consolation for doing unpleasant jobs was that they were always followed by a large undiluted dram of new spirit. At that time there was no shortage of unpleasant, manual tasks which nobody would be expected to perform today. For example, we had to empty the coal wagons that came in and barrow all our next shift's coal into the stillhouse and break up any big lumps to fire the stills. The mashtuns were emptied and cleaned by hand, which involved a team of four men who each dealt with a quarter of the tun and worked up a powerful sweat in the process.

We also had to go into the washbacks to clean them, and first we needed to make sure there was no carbon dioxide present. We did this by lowering a 'tow' – a lit candle inside an old paint tin at the end of a length of string – down into the washback. If the candle remained alight, it was safe. We stripped to the waist and used heather besoms to clean the washbacks. During the silent season we even had to go into the boiler. We would cut eye-holes in empty barley bags which we then put on, tied in place by a piece of string around the waist. We had to lie on our backs chipping off the scale on the insides with little hammers. The noise in such a confined space was incredible, and this was before ear protectors had become standard issue.

The tun room at Aultmore was interesting, because the washbacks were all old wooden ones, and on a Saturday afternoon if you weren't allowed to play rugby, you had to supervise the fermentation. That was when it was very 'busy' with the mechanical beaters going round and round controlling the froth. You were known as the 'switchy', because the beaters were called 'switchers'. We also had to peel bars of industrial soap into buckets and mix them with water, making a slimy, gooey mess. When you put this into the washbacks it acted as a surfactant and helped to inhibit the frothing as well. In those days it was the one way you could keep control. Nowadays there are more efficient inhibitors and yeasts are more stable.

Everything in the place was driven by an old steam engine, so there were fly-wheels and drive-belts everywhere. It looked just like an old cotton mill in a Lowry painting. Sometimes the belts on the switcher blades would come off due to the workload, and the washbacks would actually start to 'dance' on their bases; the wooden lids would fall off, and the wash would 'boil' out over the sides. All the while we were pouring in buckets of viscous soap mix and trying to replace the drive belts while balancing on beams above the open backs. Needless to say, that was long before Health and Safety legislation as we now know it!

When it came to the actual process of distillation, Aultmore was fortunate to have Jackie Nichol, a wild, gregarious young man, and a terribly good stillman. He taught me just about everything I needed to know about how to handle a direct-fired still. He was an expert, and knew exactly when to close the damper, when to pull the fire and when to cool it down to control the rate of distillation, so he was a tremendous influence. My own first effort at distilling was not, however, a success. At that time the science of distillation was less than precise, and the wash still at Aultmore was equipped with small wooden balls on lengths of string. The theory was that if you swung the ball against the neck of the still and it made a hollow sound everything was proceeding according to plan, as only vapour was rising into the still head. If, however, the ball made a solid sound, then the wash was rising too far up the neck of the still, and the fire had to be damped down to reduce the level of wash immediately. During my first attempt I obviously forgot some of Jackie's advice, particularly in respect of closing the dampers, for not only did the wash rise up into the still head but it flowed over and through the condenser in the worm tub before ultimately pouring out of every orifice in the spirit safe and onto the floor, bursting all the thermometers in the process!

The excise officer, Tom Pettigrew, was called, and I was far from popular, because not only was it expensive to replace the thermometers, but Charlie had to make an official report to Customs & Excise, who were also unhappy because of the potential loss of revenue. I was carpeted by Charlie and the excise officer, though, to be fair, Charlie stood up for me. 'Well, it's not the first time it's happened and I don't expect it will be the last,' he said. 'How else are we going to train the managers of the future except by letting them try things for themselves. I acknowledge, however, that it is unacceptable behaviour, and in the circumstances, to make an example and as an act of goodwill to the revenue, we are going to fine my trainee five shillings.'

I then reported back to Jackie Nichol, where I got a bigger 'doing' than I had from Charlie and the exciseman. 'You stupid bastard,' he shouted, 'I'll get into trouble next for not teaching you right,' and he, in turn, got a doing from the brewer. Afterwards, I suggested that even though I was already five shillings out of pocket, I would buy all the boys a pint, and so we went to the pub and settled our differences by getting suitably drunk. Everybody went home happy at the end of the night.

Chapter 2
Speyside:
Distillery Detective

The distilleries' inspector at that time was a Mr Mackenzie – known to everybody as Bully Mackenzie, and for very good reason. He was a huge man with a very large stomach – the sort of stomach you imagine preceding old Victorian gentlemen – and he *was* a bully. You never, ever questioned Mr Mackenzie.

One day in September 1964 he appeared at Aultmore and instructed me that as of that afternoon I would be going to Knockdhu Distillery for at least a fortnight as relief manager. The reason for this was that the manager of Knockdhu Distillery, Jimmy McQueen, was on sick leave having partaken of too much of the *cratur*. Mr McQueen had not, however, been informed that I was turning up that afternoon, so you can imagine my trepidation as a young trainee with less than a year's experience announcing to Mr McQueen that he should really be on sick leave and not in the office at all. He was officially on sick leave, but he'd come back to the office that afternoon – I think for more 'medicine'.

Almost every distillery in those days had a male clerk, and the one at Knockdhu was called Colin Mackenzie. He was a wonderful footballer who squandered his talent. He could have played in the big time, but he finished up playing for Rothes in the Highland League. Colin also was known to take a bit of a bucket. So I was going into a situation where both the manager and the clerk took a bucket or two, and I wondered who I could turn to for help. It was the brewer, as it was on many occasions, as he tended to stay at the distillery for much longer than the average manager. Knockdhu's brewer was a man by the name of Robbie Curr, a very nice guy, but not surprisingly most concerned by this complete greenhorn turning up to take control.

I approached the situation at Knockdhu with understandable trepidation, but I didn't really have too much time to think about how I was going to handle it, as I was only given an hour by Bully Mackenzie in which to prepare, and then it was just a ten-mile drive from Aultmore. I knew quite a lot about the practicalities of making whisky by this time, and I knew enough about the bookwork side of the business. I also knew what to look for if the spirit yields were not what they should be, either due to illegal extraction, bad maintenance or poor work practices. But I was still nervous.

When I arrived at Knockdhu I was probably the youngest person on the premises, but I was at an age when I had no preconceived ideas and tended to think that I knew everything I needed to know anyway. I was a brash 22 year old and just went in without too much consideration for the consequences.

One of the first things I discovered at Knockdhu, and was appalled to do so, was that the men on the shifts received no fewer than *three* quarter-bottles of the finest mature sherried malt each and every shift! Back at Aultmore dramming had consisted of two measured amounts of new spirit per shift! The tradition of 'dramming' was usually down to the discretion of the distillery manager in conjunction with the excise officer, so something of a culture must have set in. I did my best to dissuade the brewer from dishing out such large quantities, as I thought this was just plain daft. Not surprisingly, he didn't take too kindly to my idea, but he eventually agreed to restrict it to two quarter-bottles per shift during my time there. This led, however, to a near mutiny when the ration was reduced.

Knockdhu Distillery was even smaller than Aultmore. It produced about 4,000 proof gallons of spirit per week, while Aultmore made 7,000. It suffered from repeated breakdowns, nearly all connected with the chain grate stoker systems which had recently been installed. This was the first move towards modernisation away from hand-firing the stills. The chain grate stokers used to break down with monotonous regularity, because the coal had to be of a certain quality, and if it hadn't been riddled and screened properly and there were stones amongst it, these would do untold damage to the stokers. This was a completely new situation for me, and I really hadn't a clue what to do about the breakdowns. I was called out a number of nights to try to deal with this, and every single time it happened, the men seemed to require some form of persuasion of the liquid variety in order to help.

At the end of the first week, when Knockdhu closed down, I went back to Aultmore to report to John Nicol, and he in turn had to report what I said to the distilleries' inspector, Bully Mackenzie. The inspector was very disturbed when he found out about the dramming practices at Knockdhu, and it was obvious that something serious was going to have to be done about it in the near future. The brewer there was working under great pressure, with great difficulty, because he was not being supported by his manager, and it was his manager's instructions to give out such generous drams. I hasten to add that the manager was a lovely man, who knew how to make good whisky. He just admired it too much himself.

This was my first experience of what might be termed the less disciplined side of malt whisky production, far removed from John Nicol's strict methods, but in a way it was a throwback to what had gone on in the past. At that time the industry was attempting to drag itself clear of that image, which was one of the reasons I was in the company in the first place. They had never brought trainee managers in before and had always promoted from within the ranks, as it were. Some were excellent, but others just couldn't make the change. There's no doubt that in those days there was far more 'problem drinking' in the industry than there is now.

Knockdhu Distillery is on the edge of the hamlet of Knock, which I recall consisting of a post office and a pub...or maybe the drinking took place in the back of the post office. Wherever it happened, there was certainly plenty of it going on. I stayed in a local house, where I was treated very well, but one of the problems in living like that was that you were terrified of saying too much because you didn't know who was related to who, and what offence you might cause. It was the same at Aultmore, and in all such close communities.

Knockdhu was a lovely little distillery situated by the River Isla, beneath Knock Hill, in a beautiful corner of Banffshire. It was half way between Keith and the fishing port of Banff. It had a great setting and a good feel about it. I was told that during the war a unit of the Indian Army had been stationed there for some reason, and that they had created a halal slaughterhouse in one of the buildings in which to prepare their meat. Knockdhu produced fantastic whisky, which is why you now see it being marketed as a single malt by Inver House Distillers who bought it from United Distillers and sell the whisky as An Cnoc – Gaelic for 'The Hill' – to avoid confusion with the Knockando Distillery near Aberlour. Knock Hill is one of Speyside's landmarks, and is visible for miles.

Knockdhu was the first distillery to be bought by DCL, and was built during the 1890's whisky boom, when so many new distilleries were constructed. I'm told that when it opened, each member of staff was supplied with a cottage with a water closet, a feature which was by no means universal in the Highlands at that time.

The new stoking systems were the first move to modernise Knockdhu and other distilleries since the Second World War and SMD created a works department in the head office which they had recently built in Elgin. It was set up in order to effectively rebuild the distilleries. quite a number of which had not changed much since they were built in the 1890s or even earlier.

Aultmore, for example, was still doing its own floor malting, although it was also receiving malt from elsewhere. It was making about 60 percent of the total required, whereas Knockdhu had dispensed with their malt barns completely and all their malt requirement was brought in. The DCL had started to buy up family malting concerns around Scotland and they were supplying distilleries from those. They soon began buying it in from independent commercial maltsters too, as they were beginning to build specialised state-of-the-art maltings. Subsequent to that, the DCL embarked on its own maltings-building programme, and they now have a big plant at Burghead near Elgin, another nearby at Roseisle, one at Muir of Ord, and there is also one next to the old Port Ellen Distillery on Islay.

It was during the September of 1964 that I met my future wife, Kay, at a dance in The Two Red Shoes in Elgin. She came from Elgin, but was away at teacher training college in Glasgow during term time. I had previously seen her one evening after rugby training in a bar known as The Hut at the back of the Tower Hotel. It was called The Hut because it was just that – a wooden hut – and we rugby players weren't allowed into the actual hotel to drink. Then one Saturday night at the Two Red Shoes she came over and asked me to dance.

She told me that she'd seen me playing rugby a couple of times, and that she'd become interested in the game through an old boyfriend who played. She was tall, willowy and vivacious with a great sense of humour and she liked rugby. It seemed too good to be true. I joked that she must have fancied my legs, but pointed out that they weren't so impressive that night, as I could hardly stand up. She forgave me for treading on her toes while we danced, and we started going out together.

The Two Red Shoes used to attract some pretty well-known pop groups at that time – the Dave Clark Five played there once, and a regular band we really rated was Malcolm Clark and the Cresters, who came from Preston. It had all started with Albert Bonici who had a café in Elgin and built the Two Red Shoes Dance Hall. He turned into a bit of an impresario, booking bands all over the North of Scotland. One night a group we'd never heard of came up to play. Apparently they had just cut a record which was yet to be released and we weren't impressed with the look of them in their daft wee jackets, or the sound of their music. They played to about 40 people. The general concensus in Elgin was that they weren't a patch on Malcolm Clark and the Cresters, and that they should get their hair cut – we thought it just looked ridiculous. A few weeks later the record was released. It was called *She Loves You*, and the group was The Beatles. They were never asked to play Elgin again.

When I first went up to Aultmore I had a girlfriend in Edinburgh, called Dorothy, but the distance between Edinburgh and Speyside really brought that relationship to an end. Particularly in those days, it took you just about all day to make the journey. Going out with Kay wasn't really a lot easier, because although she came from Elgin, she was only there for a couple of weeks after we got together and then she was off back to Glasgow for the new term. For a while it was a toss up whether I went to Edinburgh or Glasgow to see Dorothy or Kay!

●　　●　　●

The powers that be must have been quite pleased with what I had done at Knockdhu, because just two or three weeks later I was sent to relieve at Banff Distillery, where, I was informed, there was no manager. They didn't tell me *why* there was no manager, and I just assumed he must be on holiday. I turned up on the Monday morning, walked into the manager's office and sat down. After a few minutes the clerkess of the distillery, a very matronly lady called Mrs Crummie,

walked in and said, 'How do you feel about sitting in that chair?'
I told her, 'I haven't really thought about it yet, I'm just getting a
general feel for the place.'

'You know the previous manager here shot himself?' she
responded and rather stupidly, I asked, 'Why would he do that?'

'He was very depressed,' she said, adding with a rather tragic
look in her eyes, 'As a matter of fact he was sitting in that very chair
when he shot himself.'

I jumped up from the chair and walked out of the office,
thinking what the Hell had I let myself in for here. Mrs Crummie then
asked me if I was alright, and I replied that I didn't much like the idea
of somebody shooting themselves in the chair I had just been sitting in.
And then, as though talking about some minor domestic
disagreement, she went on, 'Oh well, it's all over and done with now.
Would you like a cup of tea?' What I really needed was a large dram
of Banff to calm my nerves, but I settled for the tea, and we sat down
and talked about Banff Distillery.

It was beautifully located, just behind the sand dunes, facing
the Moray Firth. During the Second World War, Banff had had the
misfortune to be bombed – by a single German plane that had
probably been going for the docks at Aberdeen one night and got a bit
lost. The distillery men smashed open casks and poured away
thousands of gallons of spirit as the fire spread. One fireman reputedly
ended up in court for filling his helmet with whisky as it flowed past
him and sharing it with his colleagues. The spirit got into the local
drains and streams and ducks and geese were found lying inebriated
beside the distillery outflow. It was said that cows were so drunk they
couldn't be milked next day.

When I was there Banff was producing about 9,000 proof
gallons of spirit per week, so it was the biggest distillery I had been at
so far, but there was always a shortage of water there, no matter what
time of year it was, and the stills always used to run a bit hot. As a result

of that you had to be careful not to run the stills too quickly. I always thought Banff whisky was fairly ordinary, but it was produced when there was a shortage of whisky in the world and after the war they needed spirit that would blend well enough. Banff fitted that bill and it was never going to stand out as a single malt. DCL closed the distillery in 1983, and it has now been totally demolished.

Banff had chain grate stokers like Knockdhu, but they didn't seem to have the same problems, perhaps they kept a better eye on the coal being fed in and picked out the stones, a solution which never seemed to have occurred to anyone at Knockdhu. Or perhaps they just didn't have a grievance about dramming.

Banff had an exciseman called Mr MacDonald, who was the first excisemen I had come across who came to work in a kilt. Not only that, he was always accompanied by his Afghan hound. This was very much a throwback to the days when the exciseman had a position akin to that of the laird. He was approaching 60, and had been in the excise service all his days. He was very helpful, especially with any production difficulties or procedural work from the excise side which was new to me. There was no sense in him saying, 'You're from the other side, you should know,' which was the attitude of some of the old excise professionals.

He suited himself as to his work patterns, however. The spirit charge and the account of spirits and feints and low wines had to be done not to suit the distillery, but to his personal timetable. You might have been ready to take the final accounts at noon on a Friday, but if it didn't suit him to turn up until four o'clock then you just waited. The excise officer was a very powerful figure in those days.

It was Mr MacDonald who cured the problem of condensation getting into the distributor cap of my Jaguar and preventing it starting in the morning by Sellotaping a polythene bag over the distributor. He was a very practical man, despite turning up for work in a kilt accompanied by an Afghan hound.

At Banff I felt a bit like the lord of the manor. Once things were running smoothly I would go out of an afternoon and walk along the beach, which would no doubt have been frowned upon by the company, but it seemed to me that once you had got your work done and everything was running smoothly you could go off for a couple of hours. You were, after all, coming in to do night surveys, so it seemed only fair that there should be an element of flexibility.

Banff was another distillery where modernisation was being implemented, and it only malted a small amount of its barley by the time I got there. Whisky-making was always a very conservative business, even allowing for new ideas and new types of people coming into the industry. This prevented them from going all-out overnight into a new situation, which was why they carried on with on-site malting as well as bringing in external supplies of malt. If you have a decent whisky to start with, you are very mindful that any unknown factors could alter it, and the malt that was produced in the maltings at each distillery produced a particular kind of whisky and was made in a particular way – a way in which it had been made for many, many years. At that time, the analysis of producing malt, the chemistry of it, was not so advanced that you could go to an outside maltster and ask for a malt specification for a particular distillery in the way that you can today.

Prior to the late fifties, the DCL's distilleries had been monitored from the Glenochil research station near Alloa, and all their experts had been based there. When they built a new head office in Elgin they not only installed a board of directors, they also set up a complete works department, headed by people from Glenochil. It was perceived that most of the company's expansion was going to take place on Speyside, because that was where the bulk of its malt distilleries were located.

DCL also had one or two silent distilleries in the North of Scotland which became workshops, and so not only were the scientists based in the area, but the 'spanner men' were too. They formed a 'flying squad', comprising engineers, electricians, bricklayers, plasterers and masons, and this squad was based at Parkmore Distillery, on the outskirts of Dufftown. Parkmore was a real curiosity because you couldn't find it on any of the whisky maps. It had not worked since the early 1930s, although it survives unchanged today, and is still used for warehousing. All the spare parts like pumps, gearboxes, and anything that might break down in a distillery were stored there. Because the company had so many distilleries, the squad was more or less permanently on the road, and there were very few resident engineers in distilleries at that time.

If you got a blue flame in the furnace in the middle of the night it meant there must be a leak in the still. You then had to knock out the bricks of the furnace at its base, phone Ernie MacDonald, the foreman at Parkmore, and then you would stop distilling, pull the fire, and pump out the contents of the still slowly. If you did it too quickly the still would collapse in on itself. You then had to cool the still down by pumping in cold water before the Parkmore team arrived, and they would then proceed to pull the place apart!

●   ●   ●

After my time at Banff I went back to Aultmore, but it soon became apparent that I would be there only for a few weeks then sent off somewhere else. It became quite a nomadic existence, and my next posting in late October was to Teaninich Distillery at Alness, down by the Cromarty Firth. By this time they had rebuilt Teaninich and it was capable of producing 14,000 proof gallons per week. It was working at full capacity at that time, and we were having trouble finding room in the warehouses for the casks of new spirit. Teaninich was a comparatively large distillery, with four stills at that point, though they subsequently enlarged it a lot more with an additional stillhouse a few years later; the old part I knew is now mothballed. At that time all the whisky was going for blending, and most of it still is, with just a very small amount now being bottled by UDV.

The brewer there was an Englishman by the name of Eric Edmeads who had been in the RAF and decided to stay in Scotland after his service – he had been stationed at Evanton near Alness. He married a local girl and got a job in Teaninich Distillery. He was nobody's fool and he had learnt his craft well; as brewer he was effectively the assistant manager. He went on to become a very good manager for DCL. He greeted me when I arrived at Teaninich, where the manager, Willie Mackay, was on holiday (this time the manager really *was* on holiday!). He ran a very tight, disciplined ship and everything was in good order, so it was rather like being back at Aultmore. The place almost ran itself while I was there. Eventually Willie left SMD and became the production director of Old Bushmills Distillery in County Antrim, Northern Ireland.

While I was at Teaninich I was invited to go and look at Dalmore Distillery, which was almost nextdoor. This was the first time I had seen stills with such tall, slim necks and water jackets enveloping them at the top. That had the effect of cooling down the vapour in order to produce condensate which would drop back down again as refluxed spirit and strengthen the remaining liquid in the still. This resulted in a spirit of fairly high strength when it was eventually collected. It would also be a purer, less congeneric, and thus perhaps a less characterful spirit.

Ultimately, Dalmore was acquired by Whyte & Mackay, but at that time it was still privately owned by Major Mackenzie. It was my first look at a privately-owned distillery, because at that time I tended to think the whole Scottish whisky industry was the DCL, which was, of course, what they wanted you to believe.

I went back to Aultmore for the winter, but by this time the men there realised I was no longer a real rookie, and thought they should be a bit more guarded in some of their actions when I was around and in what they said to me, in case I was now on the other side, as it were.

Because of this, I thought it might be a good idea to move on from my lodgings with Nellie at Aultmore, so I went to stay at a little farm about a mile up the hill where I was a bit more divorced from the daily life of the distillery. This was fine in theory, but when I got there I found that one of the farmer's daughters was about to marry a man who worked at the distillery, so I still couldn't really get away from it.

The farmer was called Dod Farquhar, and he and his wife certainly loved their food. There was always wonderful farm cooking. The boiled beef and tatties time was gone. I got a great variety of food there: home-grown potatoes, milk straight from the cows, fresh eggs and chicken. Dod Farquhar was a man whose braces and trousers came up almost to his chin. He was a real working farmer. The first day I was there I walked up from the distillery for my lunch, which was enormous, and after the meal Dod dropped one brace off his shoulder, put one foot up on a chair and slept for about half an hour before he went back out to work. He suggested that I should do the same and that it would do me good, so I joined him. I was actually so full of food that I couldn't really do much else. The Farquhars had two daughters but no sons, and I was treated like the son they never had.

●   ●   ●

I stayed there for the rest of the time I was at Aultmore, but I was soon on my travels again – to spend a month at Balmenach Distillery. Balmenach is five miles out of Grantown, off the Aberlour road, just outside the village of Cromdale. It was a fairly sophisticated plant for its time in a setting of real grandeur at the foot of the Cromdale Hills, surrounded by heather and burns. Despite all the modernisation in the sixties, UD closed it in 1993, but Inver House Distillers came to the rescue, as at Knockdhu, and Balmenach is once again making whisky.

The Speyside railway line was still working when I was there, and it ran up the length of the Spey from Aviemore and the south.

Barley trains used to come up into Speyside to the various distilleries, and Balmenach had a 'puggie' engine which used to go down and hitch onto wagonloads of barley in a siding and bring them up and empty them into the barley silos. Coal also came in by rail, and barrels of spirit left the distillery the same way. This all went on until Dr Beeching closed the line shortly after I was there.

Balmenach had at one time been in the family of the diplomat and author Sir Robert Bruce Lockhart, who wrote the classic book *Scotch* in the early fifties. Lockhart tells the story of how his great-grandfather James Macgregor had been visited at Balmenach by an excise officer looking for illegal stills back in the 1820s. Macgregor was a farmer, and he showed the exciseman over his farm after giving him a generous dram of whisky. During the tour the exciseman pointed out a small building beside a stream and asked about its function. 'That'll just be the peat shed,' replied Macgregor. At the end of the visit Macgregor gave the officer another dram and they chatted amicably. As he took his leave, the exciseman said quietly, 'If I were you Mr Macgregor, I'd just take out a licence for yon peat-shed.' Macgregor took the hint, and Balmenach Distillery was born.

For once, I was told before I went to Balmenach what the circumstances were. I was informed that the manager, John Connan, had taken an enforced break as he was having serious marital problems and had started to hit the bottle. His assistant was called Jimmy O'Neill, who had come from Rosebank Distillery near Falkirk, and he couldn't keep off the drink either. So there was a serious problem. It felt like Knockdhu all over again.

I was told by Bully Mackenzie before I went there that whatever I did I had to keep Jimmy O'Neill out of the spirit store and out of the sample room – in fact away from drink in any shape or form. This put me in a pretty impossible position, as here was a trainee trying to tell a man with about 30 years experience to keep out of most of his own distillery. At that time there was an on-site laboratory at Balmenach as they had just installed a new type of maltings, called Saladin Box maltings. They were doing germination counts and all sorts of other tests on the malt to work out such things as what potential spirit yields might be. The Saladin maltings had just been installed at a handful of other distilleries, including Daluaine and Ord, over beyond Inverness. The advantage of pneumatic, automated Saladin maltings compared to floor maltings was that they could handle far greater quantities of barley using the same number of men. The capacity of Balmenach had been doubled during modernisation from around 10,000 gallons per week, so they had to find a way of producing more malt with which to make the spirit. Hence the Saladin maltings.

Adjoining the lab at Balmenach was the sample room, and samples were being brought in from other distilleries in the area in order to do gas chromatography analysis – something which was in its very early days then. There were spirit samples everywhere. Every now and then during my time at Balmenach I would lose Jimmy, only to find him comatose in the sample room in the afternoon. The brewer was called Tommy Edwards, and he had had to put up with all this for years. He was just resigned to the situation. I approached Tommy and asked him what he thought we should do about Jimmy O'Neill. He replied, 'Ach, don't do anything. He's been like that for years, and he'll still be here after you've gone.'

This was no doubt good advice, but unfortunately Bully Mackenzie appeared one day, and after a while he came up to me and said, 'I've been round the whole distillery John, and I can't find Jimmy O'Neill. Are you hiding him?'

'I've had to make arrangements for Mr O'Neill to be taken home this afternoon.' I replied as neutrally as I could.

'Why is that?' queried Bully.

'I think you know why, Mr Mackenzie', I replied.

'Has he been in the sample room again?' he asked. 'I made you responsible for keeping him out, why was he in there?' I pointed out that Balmenach was a large distillery and it was impossible to keep track of his movements all the time. Balmenach was then producing 21,000 proof gallons per week, so it was a big place to cover. Bully grunted and glowered, but said no more.

Despite all the modernisation that had gone on at Balmenach, the spirit yields were terribly low in relation to the rest of the group, which was basically due to slack management. There were great problems there, all personnel problems, with a lot of sloppy procedures and poor supervision. Tommy Edwards had basically given up. He had no support from management and he was getting on in years – he was counting the days until he could retire. Years later I met him and he told me, 'Balmenach was a great place when I went there, but it went down and down…don't forget, managers come and managers go, but the brewer tends to stay.' All I could do in my time there was to contain the situation, I couldn't do anything to solve the problem. Eventually the manager came back and was pensioned off early, but in order to get stability I believe they changed the whole top management of the distillery. It was inevitable really.

● ● ●

I was still playing rugby while I was based at Balmenach, and one Friday evening, after everybody had gone home, I took my kit – unwashed from the previous Saturday – into the mash house, where I cleaned it up with the power hose and then hung it up between the two heaters to dry, ready for the following day's game. I was in the act of adding my rugby shirt to the items on the makeshift washing line when the Managing Director of SMD, Mr Hastie, appeared in the mash house, making an unscheduled visit. He had been to Dalwhinnie Distillery on business, and it was his practice to call at every SMD distillery he passed on the way home for a dram. At the best of times,

Mr Hastie was not a man to use two words where one would do, and that evening he needed very few words to make his displeasure clear. It was an extremely embarrassing moment.

We used to get rid of our effluent – or pot ale – at Balmenach by pumping it up a hill in a pipe and spraying it onto what had been a heather moor. It was superb for regenerating the moor back into green grass, but eventually it ran down off the hills into the Cromdale Burn and ultimately the River Spey, and river purification boards began to get much tougher. At one time, farmers used to buy what was known as 'dreg', which was the residual leftovers from the distillation, and spread it on their fields. In effect, Balmenach Distillery was reclaiming land using this same stuff. (On Islay, all the biggest and best crabs and lobsters are reputed to be caught around the distillery outlets where pot ale is pumped into the sea.)

Eventually, Balmenach was faced with the choice most distilleries faced, which was either to tanker the waste away to a central point where it could be dealt with, or set up an effluent purification plant. At that time, distillers only processed the pot ale, not the draff as well, as they do today in what they call 'dark grains' plants. The spent grains from the mash tun used to be sold to agricultural merchants, who would tender for the contract at the start of each distilling season, and they had to make sure that their lorries were there every few hours to pick it up and take it away. Farmers used to buy the draff and feed it to their cattle through the winter. They still do, and there are some herds of cattle raised in Speyside exclusively on draff as a winter feed.

Even Aultmore had a tiny distiller's dried solubles plant, which was referred to as the Skitter House. They took the high-protein pot ale and dried it in a steam-heated drum, which 'toffeed-up' the yeasty solids contained in the spent wash or pot ale. As it cooled it formed a big wafer and was sliced up and dropped into paper bags in what was almost powder form. What they do today in 'dark grains' plants is to dry the draff or spent grains, mix the spent grains with the pot ale, and then dry the whole lot. What comes out is a much more fibrous by-product than before. It is, of course, still very high in protein.

For the month I was at Balmenach I was put up in the Waterford Hotel in Grantown-on-Spey, which was fine as it was a very good hotel, but it was very popular and didn't have too many letting rooms. One Saturday night I was asked if I could vacate my room, and they made me up a bed in the reception area. It was like sleeping in Piccadilly Circus, or rather not sleeping. There was a lovely waitress called Rachel who was very good to me while I was there, and we had long chats about this and that and sometimes at dinner she even used to give me an extra potato!

●　　●　　●

At the beginning of December 1965 I was summoned to John Nicol's office at Aultmore, and informed that I would be going to Imperial Distillery for an indeterminate period to learn about warehousing. In those days Imperial – at Carron on the Spey – was a silent distillery within the group, and at one time it had a lot of excess warehouse capacity. Whisky from other working distilleries was being taken to Imperial and stored there. It was all traditional warehousing: earthen floors and ashes, with runners, and cask rolled in next to cask. The days of multi-storey end-on-end palletising were still far in the future.

Imperial was unusual in that it had been built out of Aberdeen brick rather than the more usual stone, and today the huge red distillery chimney stands as a landmark, though it is no longer topped by a crown, as it used to be. Imperial was a huge distillery dating from the 1890's 'whisky boom', and like a number of UD plants closed in the eighties, it found a new lease of life, albeit a brief one. It was acquired by Allied Distillers, but is currently mothballed again. It is a measure of how things have changed in the industry that I believe the current manager of Imperial is also manager not only of nearby

Glentauchers but also Scapa Distillery (also silent), well over a hundred miles north – and on Orkney!

I stayed in the Archiestown Hotel, which is on the scenic route from Grantown-on-Spey to Rothes or Craigellachie, and seemed to be on top of the world. The village of Archiestown was known locally as Kabul, after the capital of Afghanistan. Archiestown is 947 feet above sea level – they even have a plaque on the village green boasting about the fact. It was originally a planned village, much like the Speyside whisky centres of Aberlour, Dufftown and Keith, and as with most things in Banffshire and Morayshire, there was a member of a branch of the Grant family behind it. There were certainly any number of them involved in distilling, and Glenfarclas Distillery, near Aberlour, is still privately owned by Grants. Apparently Archiestown was built as a settlement for weavers, but maybe there wasn't enough oxygen there for them to work! I was told by the owner of the hotel that Archiestown was a wild place and I was best to avoid the public bar and stay in the lounge.

It was the middle of winter and if there was snow anywhere you could bet it would be in Kabul. Imperial Distillery was situated almost directly at the foot of the hill, going due south from Archiestown, and there were a couple of very severe bends on it. On one of the bends there was the entrance to a very large estate which was owned by the Wills tobacco family. One morning on my way to work I ended up half way up their driveway having skidded on the bend.

The manager at Imperial was Jim Scott, and when I arrived at the distillery he said to me, 'When you get into the warehouses I would like you to keep a very weather eye on the men because I'm not too happy that everything is as it should be.' Not again, I thought, not another role as the 007 of the whisky world.

Hundreds of casks were coming in and hundreds going out, and it soon became abundantly clear to me that there seemed a lot of movement of the men in and out of the warehouse – much more than should have been necessary. I couldn't, however, see who was doing what. The men would ask me if I would go and check a cask they suspected of leaking, or something similar, and I was sure that things were happening while I was away doing that. After about a week I went into Jim's office and said, 'I think there's a real problem here, but I can't pin it down.' He told me I would have to carry on trying, but warned me that if I started walking into the warehouses and standing around they would certainly smell a rat. He asked me what I thought was going on, and I told him that I was pretty convinced there were fairly large quantities of whisky walking out of the warehouse.

It was not uncommon for distillery men to smuggle spirit out in long metal tubes which they had specially made, with an old penny soldered onto the bottom and a cork in the top. They were called dogs, though I never worked out why. They would hang them round their necks and put them down the side of their trouser legs. I wondered why, in the days before safety shoes were issued, so many of the men at Imperial were wearing wellington boots! The guys also used to have belts made, with small flasks fitted into them, just like gun belts. In some places, I believe, they used to use rubber hot-water bottles on strings too. (Further back many had special copper body flasks made, about an inch thick, which curved around their torsos and could not be detected.) They were all wearing big donkey jackets, which helped to hide the bulkiness.

During my fourth week at Imperial I had a cup of coffee with Jim Scott and said that I felt he would have to come into the warehouse sometime that week and deal with it. He replied, 'I don't want anything to happen that will make it look abnormal. Continue just the way you've been doing. I accept the whisky's moving, you accept it's moving.'

As it subsequently transpired, the men at Imperial were taking out gallons of whisky. They gave a whole new meaning to the phrase 'walking the dog.' There was a squad of about eight men, one of whom would act as a decoy and another as a look-out. It turned out that they had very flexible rubber tubes, so it was just a case of opening a cask and getting it running – like syphoning petrol from a car. There was obviously a lot of legitimate work happening at the same time, which made it even harder for me to try to keep tabs on what was going wrong. There were lots of lorries coming in delivering new fillings, and others taking whisky out for blending. There were hundreds of casks going to Johnnie Walker, to Black & White, and other blends every week, and I was in charge of all that.

I was also fairly certain by now who was taking it, who was actually walking out with it. It was a guy who was so plausible, so helpful, that ultimately he was positively unhelpful. I decided he was the ringleader. On Christmas Eve Jim Scott appeared without warning in the warehouse in the afternoon with Bully Mackenzie, and when they came in they locked the door behind them. All the workers were asked to take their jackets and their wellies off, and several of the guys were wearing flasks and dogs. Some were standing waiting for them to be filled, some were already filled. They were all marched round to the manager's office, and every single one of them was fired on the spot.

Prior to this, Jim Scott had told Mackenzie about our suspicions and that we were fairly certain who the ringleader was. Jim also knew that Bully had connections across in Aberdeenshire. Bully Mackenzie knew just about everybody in the North of Scotland, and he had got wind of the fact that whisky was being sold illegally in Alford – over towards Aberdeen – and it turned out to be our Imperial whisky. Customs & Excise officers were called in, and then everyone had to make out a written report. I had to make one to Jim Scott, who subsequently had to make his own written report to Bully Mackenzie, who made one to the production director of SMD. He then had to make a composite report to the Collector of Customs & Excise for the local area. The company had been seen to have done the right thing – nothing less than firing the men concerned would have satisfied Customs & Excise.

That was my experience of warehousing, and it was very valuable experience, because I learnt what to look for in later life with crooked warehousemen, though it was very painful at the time and I felt awfully sorry for the families of the men involved. That evening, as I drove back to Aultmore I felt relieved in a way to be leaving Imperial, as I didn't think I could have faced meeting them again.

That was one Christmas I'll never forget.

Chapter 3
Speyside:
Dailuaine

I returned from Imperial Distillery to Aultmore for Christmas, much of which seemed to be spent in the Gordon Arms in Keith. Word had spread very quickly, of course, about what had happened down at Imperial, but I never mentioned it, and the men at Aultmore never spoke about it to me. By this time we were on a slightly different footing in any case, because when John Nicol wasn't there I was running the distillery; I had moved on in a sense, and there was no problem with that. The men understood the situation and gave me my space. We never lost our respect for one another.

I sat my distillery exams early in 1966, three days of written exams based in the Aberlour Hotel, and I duly passed. I then waited for my posting, which came in July when I discovered that my first managerial position was to be as assistant manager at Dailuaine. I was sad to be leaving Aultmore, because I had learnt a lot there, made friends, and had some great times, but there was the excitement of moving on in the industry, and of my impending marriage, which was due to take place later that year. There was a lot to look forward to.

Dailuaine is situated just a couple of miles along the Spey from Imperial Distillery, and it nestles in a little wooded hollow. Looking at the distillery today, there is a lot of flat, empty ground around the plant that was all rail sidings when I was there. The railway ran just behind the distillery, and as at Balmenach, it brought in malt and coal. The railway was a great feature of Dailuaine, and we had our own little puggie engine which shunted wagons of barley and malt around. There was a spur line off the Strathspey Railway line near Imperial Distillery, and the puggie would go down there to pick up wagons dropped off by the main line train. The engine driver was called Willie Wilson, and was known as Puggie Wul. He used to 'go with the moon', as they say, and at certain times he was likely to just drive the engine at you if you were in his way.

Dailuaine was the first distillery to be fitted with the pagoda-shaped kiln roof that everyone now thinks of as a typical distillery feature. It was designed in the 1890s by an Elgin architect called Charles Doig, who became famous for the work he did on distilleries in the area, and who had also designed nearby Imperial.

When I arrived there, Dailuaine was in the process of being torn apart, expanded and rebuilt. The distillery had belonged to Dailuaine-Talisker Distilleries Ltd before DCL acquired it in the twenties. A throwback to those days was that on the brown 'standard issue' coats with which every employee was issued were the initials DTD rather than the usual SMD for Scottish Malt Distillers. Presumably the company had built Dailuaine to give them a Speyside whisky to complement Talisker from Skye for blending purposes.

Dailuaine became the biggest malt distillery in the DCL group, it was capable of producing 30,000 proof gallons of spirit per week when I was there. A lot of people used to refer to Dailuaine disparagingly as The Feints Factory – feints being the rough, impure spirit left after the 'middle cut' of good stuff has been run from the still.

At the same time as they were rebuilding Dailuaine, the company was also upgrading Cardhu, Craigellachie and Benrinnes, all of which were close by. They were actually talking of building new distilleries, and were adding new bits on to existing distilleries. Mannochmore was added to Glenlossie near Elgin, and a 'Number Two Unit' was attached to Glendullan in Dufftown. It was much easier to add on new units to existing distilleries rather than close down the plants in order to redevelop them, thereby losing valuable production.

When they were upgrading and rebuilding distilleries during the sixties and even later, DCL made some pretty terrible architectural blunders, in my opinion. When I went back to Aultmore a couple of years ago after 30 years away I was shocked to see what they had done to the place. All the old stone buildings had gone; they had slung up buildings made with pre-cast concrete blocks and flung harling stones at them. The old distilleries had been built with each process following on from building to building in a logical order, and in a lot of cases, in the days before there was much mechanical aid, gravity had been relied upon to move stuff around. I feel that in many instances the facades at least could have been left, and the insides altered. Today you would find it much harder to get away with the demolition and rebuilding, but in a curious way it mirrored what was going on in the inner-cities at the time.

When William Grant & Son increased the capacity of the old Dufftown distillery of Balvenie they just put up an asbestos-sheeted, steel-clad building; it was as if the stills had just been located in a shed at the back of the distillery. It worked well enough, but it was hardly in keeping with what the company would have had in mind when they built the neighbouring Glenfiddich Distillery in 1886/87.

Some of the new distilleries that were built from scratch on Speyside actually look much better than the ones that were 'developed'. Tormore, for example, was the first all-new distillery to be built in Scotland this century. It was conceived in the fifties, and started producing in 1959, but a lot of people felt Tormore was too great a departure from what distillery buildings were all about. It was likened to a kirk because of its big window set in the end of the stillhouse, and it wasn't long before people began to joke about two types of Holy Spirit. I think, however, that Tormore is now accepted as being a pleasant piece of architecture. No expense was spared on the project, and the distillery roof was clad in pure copper, which I seem to recall cost in the order of £40,000 – and that was 40 years ago. The whole thing set Long John Distillers back around £600,000, and in order to cut costs when it went over budget, they shaved a few feet off the plans for the distillery workers' houses.

After Tormore a new distillery was built by Justerini & Brooks at Mulben, named Auchroisk. They made a beautiful job of it, even putting in a turret with a conical roof which served no practical purpose at all, but added a lot to the general presentation of the place. Chivas Brothers also deserve praise for Braes of Glenlivet (now renamed Braeval) and Allt-a'Bhainne near Dufftown, which were built in the mid seventies. At first a lot of people didn't like them, but now they seem to blend into the landscape very well; the boldness has paid off.

When I arrived at Dailuaine, the distillery was not in production. Part of the redevelopment included putting in new steam-heated stills. The wash stills had steam kettles in them, while the spirit stills just had steam coils. They didn't actually increase the number of stills, but the object was to make everything more efficient and easier to run with more spirit being produced as a result. The warehouses filled up, and so the casks of new spirit were loaded into secure lorries each afternoon and taken off to Menstrie near Stirling, where DCL had built a huge warehouse complex so that malt whisky could be stored nearer to the blending plants.

While I was at Dailuaine, they demolished the brick chimney and replaced it with a free-standing stainless steel one. I happened to be the member of management approached by the contractors to approve the construction before they left the site. 'Approval' consisted of climbing into the bucket of their huge mobile crane along with the foreman of the erection team and being hoisted to the top of the chimney, then lowered slowly so I could inspect all the joints. My manager, John Winton, was a member of a very active distilling family. His brother George was a distillery inspector, and his nephew, also George, was a trainee with me. John had been at the bank in Aberlour getting the wages when the business with the crane started, but he arrived back in time to see me hanging out of the bucket, inspecting bits of welding a hundred feet or so off the ground. It would be a gross understatement to say he was not happy. Actually, he went berserk and insisted the men lowered me back to earth before marching me to his office and giving me a severe gutting for being so stupid when I wasn't insured to be in a bucket suspended in mid-air. You could say that even when I got back down, my feet didn't touch the ground.

Kay and I got married in July 1966, while the distillery was still silent, and we spent our honeymoon in Anglesey. She wanted to go abroad, so we did…to Wales. Unfortunately for Kay, that was World Cup year, as the English never stop reminding us, and I became engrossed in following it all on television. We were staying in a place called Bull Bay, but I wasn't much of a bull, owing to my need to watch all that football, even though Scotland hadn't even qualified.

In October of 1966 Dailuaine began producing again, but to be honest, by that time it could have been any kind of factory – it was certainly not a pretty distillery. It wasn't meant to look pretty, however. It was built to produce malt spirit in quantity, primarily for blending purposes.

Everyone was waiting with bated breath to see how it would work when we restarted, and whether the whisky it produced would differ from before. Bated breath is an apt phrase, because as soon as production began we had a major problem with ether fumes. Every time you went into the stillhouse the men had tears streaming down their faces. I'd heard about people crying into their beer, but this was ridiculous. We had put in two new washbacks during the refit, which tended to lengthen the time it took for fermentation to take place. In those days we used a mixture of pure culture yeast, solid pressed brewers' yeast and barrels of liquid yeast. Also, the distillation process had changed, in as much as we now utilised steam coils for heating, and we were pre-heating the wash for the first time, whereas before it had just slowly heated up from the temperature at which it left the washbacks. It turned out that we were using malted barley as soon as it came off the kiln – in effect it was simply too hot. All these factors put together created the ether problem. The company's chemists were called in, and the eventual outcome was that we had to alter our methods of handling the malt, we changed the yeast mix, and we started to use the stills in a slightly different way.

As assistant manager at Dailuaine, I was responsible for much of the day-to-day running of the distillery, organising shift patterns, and latterly doing much of the paperwork which the manager then double-checked before submitting it to head office in Elgin. I had a lot more responsibility than before, and, ironically, out of 35 members of staff, I was the second-lowest paid.

One of the men who worked in the tun room at Dailuaine was called Donald Bremner, and he was fairly hooked on alcohol; to the extent that he was not averse to helping himself to the 'Joe' from the washbacks. Donald was also dedicated to cutting costs in his domestic life, and he had a habit of picking up all the old cork bungs from the cooperage and putting them into bags. Nobody thought much about this, until one night the chimney of his cottage caught fire and a blue spirit flame was seen coming out of the top. That was when we realised he was using the cork bungs as fuel. The Aberlour fire engine was summoned, manned by part-timers and led by Johnny Milton, resplendent in his white Fire Master's helmet. They fitted the standpipe into the ring main, fitted the hoses, put the ladder up to the chimney, and pointed the hose down the chimney. Johnny had a lisp, and shouted, 'Right boysh, scoosh your hoshesh'.

Nothing came out.

There was no water in the ring main and probably hadn't been for years. Nobody had ever thought to test it. It ended up with the firemen filling buckets of water from Donald's kitchen sink, running outside, passing the buckets up the ladder, and pouring them back down the chimney. Needless to say after that incident a directive came down from DCL forbidding employees from burning cork bungs in distillery cottages.

Ricky Robertson – he of the Revolving Room – featured in a rugby-related episode during the early days of my marriage when I was at Dailuaine Distillery. After a match in Elgin we were a bit late getting home. I'd told my wife that I would be back by six o'clock, but it was actually ten when we reached Dailuaine. Ian Marland from Balmenach Distillery was with us, and he came in for a few drinks before we decided to give him a lift home to Balmenach, about 20 miles distant. Ian had us in for a dram there, and then we set off home, only for my Beetle to run out of petrol. It free-wheeled half way up the far side of a hill near Dailuaine, then we had to get out and push it to the road end at the top of Dailuaine Brae. Once we got it rolling from there I leapt in and Ricky chased on foot, finally jumping onto the running board as we went flying down Dailuaine Brae with no power and up into the village where we were met by our respective wives who were far from amused by the situation. It took about a week before either of them spoke to us again although Ricky and I couldn't really see what all the fuss was about.

It might seem that we spent an inordinate amount of time drinking and partying but I should say that during the week we worked extremely hard in a very disciplined way, and the drinking and partying were the sort of 'release' any group of fit, healthy young men would naturally indulge in during their leisure time.

One Hogmanay when I was at Dailuaine – in 1966 or 1967 – a few of us decided to have a meal in a restaurant at Craigellachie, overlooking the River Spey. We saw in the New Year there, then somebody said that there was a party up in Glenlivet, so off we went. We all got into our cars and headed up into the glen, on roads that were just sheets of ice. On the way there, just out of Dufftown where the road starts to get wild as it runs beneath Ben Rinnes, we came across a body lying in the road. Our first thought, of course, was that he'd been hit by a car, but on closer examination it turned out he was fine, he'd just been celebrating Hogmanay too enthusiastically, and had somehow dozed off in the middle of the road. We picked him up and put him to one side, then carried on to the party which was at a croft up beyond where the Braeval Distillery was to be built in the seventies.

The area was known as Braes of Glenlivet, and it really was a very remote spot. No doubt, the way things were, if the distillery had been there at that time, we'd have dropped in and had a dram with the brewer. The party was being hosted by a Mr Macdonald, who welcomed us in, even though it was around 2am by this time. He was cooking a side of pork on a spit over an open fire in the croft kitchen, and kept going round with a bottle of whisky in one hand, dispensing drams, and a big fork with lumps of roast pork in the other. He had salted the pork pretty thoroughly, so more drams were needed to quench the thirst, and so it went on. All night. We skidded back down the road to our various abodes some time during the afternoon of 1st January. By then, the comatose body by the roadside had gone. The man had obviously woken up at some point and made his way home too, but he couldn't have felt rougher than we did, even if he'd been out all night.

The puggie engine was quite a feature of Dailuaine, and we even got trainspotters coming to photograph it from time to time. One day we were approached by *Lui*, a French magazine we had never heard of, which wanted to use the engine in a photo shoot with some fashion models. I was put in charge of organising the event, and Puggie Wul got the engine all polished up for the day. The crew duly turned up with the girls wearing full-length fur coats on what I thought was quite a mild day. Soft French lassies, I thought. 'Are you wearing those coats because you're feeling the cold?' I asked one of them who had climbed on to the front of the engine. She smiled at me and then pulled her coat open to reveal that she was completely naked underneath. The girls from the distillery office thought this was absolutely disgusting and went and locked themselves in their office. As they were retreating, I noted that the men were leaving their posts in great haste, abandoning the stillhouse, the maltings, the dried solubles plant and every other bit of the distillery to come and watch. Geordie Davidson, who worked in the cooperage, was so excited by this turn of events that he pulled a cask from the bottom of the pile in error, and the rest of the heap rolled all over the yard. A few even ended up in the burn and found their way into the Spey.

My wife chose that precise moment to walk into the yard to see what all the fuss was about. My protestations that nobody had told me *Lui* was *that* sort of publication were clearly not believed. There were some long silences at home that evening. This was the swinging sixties, but nothing much swung around the Aberlour area – at least not until that day – so the excitement and outrage (according to gender) was not surprising. A while after all this happened, we did get to see the published photographs in *Lui*, and I have to admit it was quite a good feature. When we showed the pictures to Puggie Wul he studied them carefully for a while, then said, 'Aye, the engine looks well, right enough.'

●   ●   ●

While I was at Dailuaine, John Winton was promoted, and our new manager was Jack Dorrat, who had been manager at Speyburn Distillery near Rothes, and then at Cardhu. Jack was keen to have a good community spirit among the Dailuaine staff and their families, and so he suggested organising a Christmas dinner dance in the village hall at Archiestown, which was a couple of miles up the hill. Archiestown, of course, was up the hill from everywhere.

The dinner dance duly happened, with Bully Mackenzie and his wife as guests of honour. By this stage, the breathalyser had come into being, so we had hired a bus to allow everybody to get suitably refreshed. Unfortunately, some of the men got too well refreshed, and all the resentments and undercurrents of discontent that you find in any small, close-knit community came to the surface. Somebody had remembered that a colleague hadn't cleaned up as he should have done in the stillhouse, and that he had been forced to do the job for him when he came on to work the next shift. It didn't seem to matter that this had occurred seven years previously. Suddenly fists and pieces of village hall furniture were flying – Bully Mackenzie shepherded the ladies from the top table out of the back door to safety while Jack Dorrat and I tried to calm things down, aided by the local constabulary. Eventually everybody walked, staggered or was carried into the bus for the short but tense drive home. The police agreed not to press charges, provided the damage was paid for, which saved much embarrassment all round. I don't think the company would have been overly impressed to read all about it in the *Northern Scot*. That was the first, and I have to say the last, of the Dailuaine Distillery dinner dances with which I was associated.

I wasn't entirely immune from the petty irritations of life in small communities myself. There were about 25 houses in Dailuaine village, and Kay and I lived in one of them. Our neighbour was a stillman named Sandy Milne. He was a very small man. My mother would have described him as 'two bricks and a teapot high'. Sandy had an immaculate garden which he had tended obsessively for about 20 years. He had a habit of coming out every time I went into my garden, saying things like, 'Let me see your neeps. Och, my neeps are way bigger than those.' This went on with a variety of vegetables until one evening when the subject was cabbages, I lost my temper and threw a quite small cabbage at him. He thought such behaviour was totally uncalled for, and proceeded to report me to the manager. Jack Dorrat considered this conduct unbecoming a distillery assistant manager, but admitted that he would probably have done the same, as Sandy had a reputation among the rest of the workforce for being tiresomely fussy and precise.

One of the two excise officers at Dailuaine was Sid Roberts. Sid was a nice man, but there was one serious drawback to him. His abiding passion in life was the snowy owl. He even built a hide in trees near the distillery in order to study the objects of his fascination at closer quarters. One evening he and his wife invited Kay and I along to their house for dinner. After a large meal, Sid sat us down with a dram each beside a roaring coal fire and uttered the ominous words, 'And now John, I'm going to show you the snowy owl.' We were then treated to about two hours of slides of the snowy owl. Standing on one leg, standing on two legs, looking sideways, looking backwards – you name it, we saw a picture of the snowy owl doing it. Kay managed to feign polite interest through the entire performance, but I let the side down badly by falling sound asleep and snoring very loudly. Sid brought the show to an end when my head was lolling dangerously close to the fire, and Kay had had to pull me upright by my tie. We were never invited again, and I can't say I had any serious regrets about that. I later discovered that he subjected everybody to that slide show, and that I was by no means the first one to fall asleep during it.

Dailuaine's second excise officer was Ray Lyons, who was extremely good at his job, but who took a serious bucket. He habitually brought his dog to work with him; an Irish Wolfhound called Seamus. He always arrived early in the morning to take the whisky charge and take account of the spirit. Eventually I realised that he arrived early so that he could put the new spirit into the coffee he brought in a flask. As the day wore on the sample tube kept being emptied, Ray's eyes became more glazed and his glasses slid further and further down his nose. Eventually he would call for Seamus, and it became obvious why he brought the dog to work. He needed something to hang onto on the steep path from the distillery up to his house.

One day I came out of the filling store, leaving Ray Lyons in there to finish his 'coffee', and discovered the brewer, Donny Mackenzie, pinned to the wall by Seamus. 'For God's sake get this bloody monster off me,' he shouted. 'My bitch is in heat and he must be smelling it off me. I think he's about to give me one!'

I shouted for Ray to come and call the dog off, but Ray was at the stage where he could hardly speak so I had to get a couple of men to help me move the dog off Donny. Having eventually managed this, we shut it in the office with Ray until it was time for the pair of them to tackle the path home.

All afternoon, as Donny passed by the office he heard the sounds of passionate paws scratching at the door accompanied by the deep resonant snoring of an inebriated exciseman.

Chapter 4
Speyside:
The Grants of
Glenfiddich

In early 1968 I applied to William Grant & Sons of Dufftown for the job of manager at their Balvenie Distillery, the sister plant to Glenfiddich, because I was interested in gaining experience outwith DCL, the giant in the industry. I wanted to get into the situation where there weren't so many boffins backing me up, and where I had to do a bit more problem solving on my own.

I was fortunate enough to be appointed, and began work there in February. The move meant a salary increase of the princely sum of £200 per year, a decent enough amount in those days. I also got a totally rent-free house, with coal and electricity paid for too. At that time those sort of things were not tax-deductible, so they were worth quite a lot.

As you approached Dufftown from the Craigellachie side, Dufftown almost was William Grant's. As well as Glenfiddich and Balvenie distilleries and all the associated warehousing, they owned two farms close by, Westerton Farm and Balvenie Mains. The company grew barley on these farms; some of it went for feeding stuffs, but a proportion was always held back for malting. This was really a throwback to the early historical beginnings of distilling, and somehow seemed appropriate to a family-owned company which had been involved with Glenfiddich Distillery since it was built in 1886/87 and Balvenie since its founding five years later. When William Grant built Glenfiddich Distillery it was the first to be constructed in Dufftown since Mortlach more than 50 years before, and was the first of the 'new wave' of late-Victorian distilleries that grew up in and around the town. At one time, William Grant, the founder of the company, had been employed at Mortlach, working his way up to become distilleries manager.

Having had all the back up of the SMD works department and technical people in Elgin, what I had now become part of was the nucleus of a management team in Dufftown. As well as the managers of Glenfiddich and Balvenie distilleries, there was a Distilleries Manager, who was effectively a general manager, and he reported to the board in Glasgow. He was Duncan Stewart, who had been promoted to that job from the role of manager at Balvenie, which was why I had been recruited.

Our new house was called Balvenie Gardens, though actually it was situated closer to the DCL distillery of Convalmore than it was to Balvenie. Convalmore is now closed, but UD sold it to William Grant & Sons a few years ago, and it is now used for warehousing their stocks of maturing whisky.

When we moved from Dailuaine, we arranged for an Elgin removal contractor called Anderson and England to take everything across to Balvenie. We bemoan the loss of railways, and the way distilleries made use of them, but the day we moved I heartily wished the railway had never come to Speyside. Not far – but far enough – from the distillery manager's house we were to occupy was a railway bridge. A bridge which was a least a foot lower than the removal lorry. Fortunately the driver realised this in time, and stopped. Unfortunately, the torrential rain which accompanied our move didn't. We got hold of a tractor and trailer, and hastily began to transfer the contents of the van onto the trailer, taking our goods and chattels along to the house load by load. This went on all day, and was hardly the ideal start to our time at Balvenie.

Although Grants was a family firm, and very much smaller than DCL, a lot of changes had already been made in their distilleries when DCL was just beginning its programme of modernisation. Quite a few of the independent distillers had been less conservative in their desire to make changes than DCL had, and Grants had become involved in fuel conservation and water recycling. When I joined the firm, the plants were already very efficient, with steam distillation, pre-heating and re-use of hot water, and there was an ever-present desire to improve efficiency and cut costs pervading the management.

Very early on in my time at Balvenie, I was called on to improve the distillery yields. In those days we measured the efficiency of a distillery in terms of proof gallons per bushel – the number of proof gallons of spirit you could produce for every bushel of malt mashed. When I went to Balvenie, the average was around 2.82, whereas SMD had in some instances been hitting 2.9, which was the magic figure to aim for at that time. Neither Glenfiddich or Balvenie had ever achieved 2.9, but by juggling ratios of water to malt and various other factors, we hit the magical 2.9 at Balvenie. It is on record that when the first spirit flowed from Balvenie in the spring of 1893, 435 gallons of whisky were produced from 200 bushels of malt, which gives a yield of 2.175. (It is also on record that William Grant bought a second-hand still from Laphroaig for his new distillery and paid £47 for it!)

Everyone was delighted when we achieved 2.9 at Balvenie, and I was invited down to the company headquarters in West George Street in Glasgow with my wife. We were given a tour of head office, which I had never seen, and taken out to lunch by the company secretary before being presented with a case of Standfast – the name of Grant's blended whisky in those days. I had never been used to this sort of treatment at DCL, and I was actually quite impressed by it all.

Balvenie had four stills in the main stillhouse, but when they expanded they had added a second stillhouse at the back which contained another pair of stills. The distillery was capable of producing 28,000 proof gallons of spirit in a seven-day week, which made it a sizeable operation when you consider that the biggest malt distillery in the SMD group was Dailuaine, which was producing 30,000 gallons on the same basis.

Virtually no Balvenie was being sold as a single malt then, but a big push to market Glenfiddich as a 'single' whisky was really beginning to take off when I was with the company. They had started a few years before, selling it as a ten year old, then they changed it to an eight year old, and I remember them going from a round bottle to the now famous triangular green bottle, with the black label and the stag's head. Glenfiddich is Gaelic for 'Valley of the Deer'. Standfast had always been sold in a clear triangular bottle, which gave them the idea to market Glenfiddich using the same shape. The name Standfast comes from the Grant clan slogan, 'Standfast, Craigellachie!' In 1969 the Glenfiddich visitor reception centre was opened in the old malt barns. I believe it was the first such reception centre in the entire Scottish distilling industry.

Grants set-up at Dufftown was as close as possible to being self-sufficient, and included a full-blown cooperage where they made and rebuilt casks, and a copper shop operation, where they fabricated and repaired all the stills for Glenfiddich and Balvenie. There was a lot of work for them, as Glenfiddich was expanding significantly during the time I was with Grants. Eventually, they had something like 32 stills. It was a great sight to see guys pummelling away at great sheets of copper, watching them gradually shaping them into stills. The noise in the copper shop was absolutely deafening, and, of course, there were no ear protectors in those days.

Grants also had their own transport fleet, along with their own painters, plasterers, stonemasons, joiners and electricians, not to mention their own bottling plant, where Glenfiddich was bottled, as it still is today. I think Springbank in Campbeltown is the only other distillery still bottling on the premises. It was a very small operation at the time, and they could only bottle something like one thousand cases per week, even working overtime.

That was my first introduction to bottling, because although I was manager of Balvenie, from time to time I would relieve the bottling manager Bobby Craig so that he could have time off. You had to be able to do everything, and there were no assistant managers. I was working day and night at times, as not only were you involved with the production, but you had all the administration to deal with, along with PR work. Despite the workload, however, I liked the fact that there was more to being a distillery manager there than had been the case with DCL.

All the casks, both Balvenie and Glenfiddich, were filled at Glenfiddich at that time in one big filling store. The Balvenie production was tanked up to Glenfiddich in an articulated vehicle, which was reversed into a bay, and there were outlets in the tanker so that the spirit could be piped directly into casks, so they didn't even have to transfer it into another vat. Once filled, the casks were taken back down the road to Balvenie's warehouses. From there the casks would eventually go down to Paisley, where the blending was done.

Being a family company, the Grants were very loathe to tell staff they had to retire when their working lives were really at an end. The old head maltman was called Willie Gill, and he had been there man and boy for more than 60 years. His son, Jimmy, was in his mid-forties and was the mashman. Technically, Willie wasn't the head maltman any more, Alex Stephen had the job, but Willie turned up for work in the malt barns each morning, and everybody still saw him as the head man. It can't have been easy for Alex, but that was the way the company worked.

What kept Willie going was coming in to work and having his dram when he started, being in the kiln turning the malt along with the rest of the staff, and having his dram mid-morning and mid-afternoon. Obviously, that couldn't have happened with a company like DCL, which had compulsory retirement at 65.

Willie Gill was as chirpy as Alex Stephen was taciturn. Maybe Alex was frightened to open his mouth in case he got told he didn't know how to do anything. Willie was a very gregarious old boy, and because of his age and the length of time he had spent with the company, he was able to tell you all about the Grant family. He could remember Charles Grant-Gordon and Sandy Grant-Gordon going into the maltings as boys, and how he made them turn the malt and worked them hard, taking no backchat, even though they were the boss's sons. When I was there Charles and Sandy Grant-Gordon were joint MD's of the company, but they would chat away to Willie when they came up from Glasgow, and it was obvious that they genuinely respected the man.

Although Grant's Dufftown set-up was very self-sufficient, they did have to buy in malt, because there were no maltings at Glenfiddich, and the floor maltings at Balvenie were small. They were really just kept so that the company could say they still did their own malting. You can still see the big silos at Dufftown station, close to Balvenie, where malt used to be brought in from commercial maltsters by rail; nearly all the malt brought in there went to Glenfiddich.

During 1968 and 1969 Grants were bottling as much Glenfiddich as a single malt as the entire distillery had produced in 1950, which goes to show the extent to which Grants had spotted the potential market for single malts and was exploiting it before anyone else. Their marketing has been absolutely superb, and it's very impressive that they have held the markets they captured early on, despite all the competition in more recent years. Glenfiddich remains the best-selling single malt in Britain and overseas. Wherever you mention whisky, Glenfiddich is the one malt everyone has heard of.

As well as my involvement with Balvenie and Glenfiddich, I also became involved with Grants' Ladyburn and Girvan operations. Girvan was their grain whisky plant, which had opened in 1963, and was part of the company's self-sufficiency strategy. Ladyburn was a small malt whisky-making unit which was added later at Girvan. Ladyburn was fully-automated, the first such distillery in Scotland, I believe. There was a major problem, however, as it was not achieving anything like the same results in terms of yields as either of the Speyside distilleries.

After we had beaten the production records at Balvenie, I was sent down to try to find out what was wrong at Ladyburn. One of the difficulties was that everything was pre-set and electronically controlled from one central console panel, which made it pretty well impossible to make any changes.

The second week I was down there, I applied to Alistair Murray, the production director in Glasgow, for permission to de-automate Ladyburn. Alistair had been distilleries manager at Dufftown before Duncan Stewart, and it was his promotion to Glasgow that had set in train the staff movements that led to me joining the company. My request was greeted with raised eyebrows and raised hackles from the men who had claimed automation was the way forward and who had set Ladyburn up. I was told de-automating it would not help the problem.

However, I persevered and we switched it onto manual control and did things the way I'd been trained to do them. We managed to get the yields up from the 2.70s into the mid to high 2.80s in a period of about five or six weeks. We were able to prove that the distillery was capable of achieving that level of yield by de-automating and going back to the human element.

When I returned to Dufftown from Ladyburn they re-automated it, and the yields plummeted again. Ladyburn went on for a number of years like that, before it ceased production in 1976. It produced a fairly reasonable Lowland malt, which was fine for blending purposes, its principal function.

As well as making whisky at Girvan, there was also what was known as the 'Gin Palace', where they compounded gin and vodka. In those days you weren't allowed to compound gin on the same site as you produced grain whisky or even neutral spirit. Grants therefore built a fence between the grain distillery and the Gin Palace, which was ridiculous, but complied with the regulations. When they wanted to make gin they just pulled neutral spirit off the stills in Girvan grain distillery and took it in tankers through a gate in the fence into the Gin Palace.

Girvan seems an unlikely site for a distillery in some ways, but it was quite close to where Grants' blending and bottling operations were, and I think they also received incentives to site it there. A lot of the mines in Ayrshire were being closed down at the time, and alternative sources of employment were being encouraged to locate in the area. Many of the men who worked at Girvan Distillery had worked in the pits before that. Grants also built a cooperage and a big warehousing complex, so there would be upwards of a hundred people working for the company in Girvan at that time.

The General Manager at Girvan was Frank MacNaughton, who had previously been distilleries manager in Dufftown, and he had been working under tremendous pressure to get Girvan up and running and hitting targets. He was a chemical engineer by training, and was an extremely nice man and a very good manager in his time, but he had taken to the bottle in a serious way under the pressure of work. Grants were extremely patient and good with him, even sending him away on a cruise to try to get him sorted out. The assistant manager was Stewart McBain, who later joined Chivas Brothers, and he was virtually running the place. He was having terrible problems with Frank, who was locking himself in his office and sleeping all day. It was a very difficult situation. Stewart was also a chemical engineer, an ex-DCL boffin from Glenochil.

Girvan was a valuable experience for me, as it was my first chance to get to know how grain distilleries worked. While I was at Ladyburn, I found time to look at the grain operation, and became interested in making grain spirit and neutral spirit. This was also my first introduction to seeing how gin and vodka were compounded.

The six weeks I spent at Girvan were hard work, and although I got to play the odd round of golf, I was not there for the good of my health. I was there to sort out the Ladyburn problems and also, I assume, to confirm what Stewart McBain may have been reporting back to higher authorities about Frank MacNaughton. I remember being well and truly pumped by my bosses later about what was going on there.

There were five Customs & Excise officers attached to William Grants in Dufftown, and the ones I came into contact with most often at Balvenie were Ron Pickthall and Harry Carrington, known to one and all as Harry Carry. The two of them used to spend many an afternoon ostensibly testing instruments. They would go into warehouses and draw samples, which they then took into their office to use for testing instruments. They would be there for the rest of the afternoon, and if you ventured in the air would be thick and blue with cigarette smoke – playing cards were always in evidence. By five o'clock the sample tube would usually be at least half-empty.

Ron Pickthall used to fancy himself as a bit of a horseman, and where Kay and I lived in Balvenie Gardens was just across a field from the distillery. Unbeknown to us, there was a right of way through the garden, and one evening we were having our tea when we saw Pickthall riding side-saddle across 'our' property, followed by an entourage of young Pickthalls.

I went out and said to him, 'What the hell do you think you're doing?' He'd been testing instruments that afternoon, so he was slurring his words slightly and was definitely on his high horse, as it were, as he replied, 'What do you mean, what do I think I'm doing. I'm riding on a right of way, where I'm entitled to be. Don't you know that? Now don't be awkward, step aside.'

'Step aside?', I echoed in disbelief, 'I'll do no such thing.'

'I'll have you know', he continued, 'that I was in the yeomanry during the war, and I was a junior officer and a gentleman.' Clearly he fancied himself still at the head of his troop. I replied, 'Well I was never a junior officer and I'm certainly not a gentleman, so get the hell out of my garden.' He left, grudgingly, saying over his shoulder as he did so, 'You'll pay for this.'

And sure enough, at work he put every obstacle he could in my way, until we came to an accommodation. I agreed that he could use the short cut through my garden, provided he closed the gate behind him, which he hadn't done on the first occasion, and provided he kept his children out of it.

By contrast with Ron Pickthall, Harry Carry was a blunt Yorkshireman, and as unpretentious and unaffected a man as could be. Everything was 'bugger' this and 'bloody' that. One afternoon he and I were taking an account of spirit on the tanker before it went up to Glenfiddich; we were inside the little hut where you could shelter from the weather and work out figures. We'd just finished when a cat lowped up onto the desk and walked across his paperwork, leaving muddy paw marks all over it. Harry had obviously been testing the instruments earlier that afternoon, because he turned to the offending animal and shouted, 'Puss off Pissy.'

Each of the five excise officers had a house, three of which were at Balvenie. One day, after extensive instrument testing, Ron Pickthall summoned me to his house and showed me some patches of damp, saying that he was not prepared to subject his wife and children to such conditions just to cut costs for William Grant & Sons. Part of the problem was that he took great exception to a young man like me having a better house than him. I hadn't been in the yeomanry, far less an officer, yet he had fought in the war for the likes of me, and there I was living in a better house than him…it just wouldn't do and so on and on he went until he ran out of reasons for complaining.

At Balvenie we had three painters. Harry Mercer was the senior of the two who actually painted, while Gordon McMahon was the junior. Gordon had flaming red hair and a temper to match. Fred Allan was their labourer, the one who mixed up the paint, thinned it down and took it to the others. This always seemed to take an eternity, and Harry was one of those painters who would go over the same bit time after time until it was just perfect. They had it figured out that if they worked at a very steady pace they could paint the whole of Balvenie and Glenfiddich in two years and then start at the beginning again. Fred and Harry were commonly known as Thunder and Lightning because of their less than prodigious work rate. Fred's other job was to clean out the fireplace in my office every morning, and his reward for doing this was a wee dram from a gallon bottle of whisky with a little tap at the bottom which I kept in a treble-locked cupboard.

Also on the Balvenie staff was a labourer called Jock Backies, who used to work between the outside squads and the malt house. He was a man in his early sixties, and he got his nickname 'Backies' partly because he had a bit of a hunchback, and partly because he rolled his own cigarettes and was always on the lookout for tobacco. If there was ever any trouble around, Jock was in it. If someone was up a ladder painting and Jock was holding the ladder, you could bet your bottom dollar the paint pot would fall on his head. He was just one of those guys.

My experience with the warehousemen at Imperial Distillery stood me in good stead at Balvenie, because exactly the same thing happened, and the whole squad had to be sacked. The warehousemen's hut was opposite the front door of my office, and I became aware of an increasing flow of traffic in and out of that hut. Although, strictly speaking, I shouldn't have done it, one Friday when the hut was empty I popped in and opened a thermos flask in a lunch bag. It may have had tea in it when the owner clocked in, but now it was full of whisky. I checked a second and a third, and there was not a drop of tea to be found.

I told Duncan Stewart what I had discovered, and he asked me to phone him the following morning once I was certain there would be some 'evidence' in the hut. Just before the squad went back to the hut at 12 o'clock for lunch I locked the door and phoned Duncan. He came down to find the men gathered around the hut waiting for their lunch. Duncan and I went in and asked them to identify their bags and flasks. When they had, Duncan said simply, 'The whole lot of you are sacked. You know what for.' All six of them just put on their coats and walked away. There wasn't a word out of any of them. This, however, created a problem, because we had no warehouse squad for Monday, and so Thunder and Lightning and various other dynamic figures were drafted in to work in the warehouse until we could recruit a new squad.

During the silent season, in the summer of 1969, we did quite a lot of work in the stillhouse over a very busy two-week period when we re-routed pipes from the stills through the spirit safes into the receivers. We began mashing again on the Wednesday, with the first mash ready for distillation on Saturday. We couldn't start distilling on Saturday afternoon as planned, however, because our coppersmiths hadn't completed the work, so it was ten o'clock at night before they announced they were finished, and distilling began. One of the stillmen was Norman McLeod, a very dapper man, and the sort of person who claimed to have been there, seen it and done it…better than anyone else.

Due to the fact that I had no assistant at Balvenie I had a phone by my bedside and at 3am on Sunday it rang. Kay came to before I did and on picking up the receiver heard an unannounced voice screaming, '*It's the fucking feints, they're pouring out like hell all over the bloody place!*'

'I think this is for you,' she said, coolly, and handed me the phone. The tidings were repeated to me. 'Norrie, what precisely *is* the problem?'

'Oh…it's yersel,' Norrie replied, 'was that your wife? Sorry. Well it's the *FUCKING FEINTS!* Can you get over here? Now?'

I did and discovered that in their haste to finish, the coppersmiths had forgotten to reconnect the pipe going into the feints receiver vat. The receiver room was literally filling up with feints. There was only one thing to do; I had to call out Ron Pickthall and Harry Carry because of the implications of the loss of spirit for the excise. Cleaning up and sorting it all out and filling in various forms took the rest of the night, and it all ended up with me having drams with Ron Pickthall and Harry Carry in the excise office at six o'clock in the morning, before we all got back to our beds. Fortunately it was a Sunday, so I was able to get some sleep, though I had to be on duty by 10am, despite it being the Sabbath.

On many occasions I was called out in the middle of the night, yet was expected to be at work again at 8am. This was one of the drawbacks of not having an assistant, and it got to be quite a problem. When you are on call seven days a week, 24 hours a day, it gets to you eventually, and I asked if there was any chance of obtaining some help. This was refused on the grounds that I should be able to do everything myself. The fact was, however, that for most of the time I was permanently exhausted. I began to take migraine attacks every few weeks and my doctor wasn't surprised when I told him that sometimes I was working 80 or 90 hours a week.

There was very little home life; very little life of any kind outside work. I even had to give up my beloved rugby. When I first went to Balvenie I still tried to play, but I didn't get the time to train, so I was becoming more and more unfit. I played on Saturdays when

I could, but it took me a week to recover. During one game I got my nose broken for the third time. I ended up in Foresterhill Hospital in Aberdeen, where I was detained overnight because they thought I also had concussion. When I got home, Kay had put my rugby boots out in the bin with the rubbish. The point was not lost on me. By the time I found out about it the boots were on the refuse tip, and with hindsight it was definitely for the best.

Although Dufftown was the capital of distilling on Speyside, I hardly had time to take much notice of what was happening in the town and at other distilleries, because my nose (barring fractures) was so close to the grindstone at Balvenie. Dufftown then had four other distilleries operating in addition to Glenfiddich and Balvenie. Close by, there was Convalmore, which belonged to DCL, as did Mortlach and Glendullan, while Arthur Bell & Son's Dufftown Distillery was also in the town. Glendullan had been the last distillery to open in Dufftown in the 19th century, coming on stream in 1897, and its construction prompted the rhyme, 'Rome was built on seven hills, and Dufftown stands on seven stills.' A few years after I left, Bells added Pittyvaich alongside their Dufftown plant, and in the early 1990s Grants built a new distillery next to Balvenie, which they have called Kininvie.

Living right on the edge of the town, we never became all that involved in the community, although Kay did get a job teaching in the local primary school. Her parents lived in Elgin, which was the main shopping centre for the area, so we tended to go there in what little spare time I had. From my standpoint, there didn't seem to be much contact between the different distilleries, unlike Islay, as I was to discover later, where everyone helped one another. I never once met the manager of Dufftown Distillery while I was at Balvenie, I never even met the manager of Convalmore, and he lived practically next door to me. The only other distillery manager I did meet was Bob Mitchell from Glendullan, and that was only the once.

The bottom line about Balvenie was that it was excellent

experience for me, but it wasn't much of a life and I certainly don't regret going there. However, I couldn't have put up with it for much longer than I did. It was interesting to note that when I left, my replacement, Ted Allan, was given an assistant! Although the company had moved forward on the technical side, in terms of the way they organised their human resources, particularly at distillery management level, they didn't seem to have realised that with distilleries working seven days a week, rather than four or five as previously, the managers needed more support and back-up.

Charles and Sandy Grant-Gordon ran the company, and it was Charles who had had the inspiration to build Girvan grain distillery, which became his pet project. Charles was an eccentric, to put it kindly, and he set up a caravan on site down there so that the men couldn't slack. One day when they had been laying a concrete floor, he decided it hadn't been done properly, so he just walked straight across the top of it in his wellington boots. The next morning, Charles came out of his caravan, and couldn't find the bike he used to cycle round the site on. 'Where's my bicycle?', he demanded of a passing workman. 'Up there', was the reply. Charles looked up and saw that they had welded his bike to the top of a steel gantry about a hundred feet high. He left the concrete alone after that.

The first time I met Charles he turned up unannounced one Saturday at Balvenie, just as I was about to go for my lunch and demanded a tour of the distillery. He didn't like what he saw at all, and said, 'Take a note of the fact that we should get rid of this grist bin, McDougall, and that heat exchanger over there.' By the time we'd finished the tour we had just about resurveyed the entire distillery. I told him that I'd already requested a replacement for the old wooden grist bin, but had been told there was no money available for one. 'Well in that case,' he said, 'make sure that before it falls down there's a mash in it, so that it goes into the mash tun.' When he left I was rather worried about everything he had said, and on the following Sunday I got hold of Duncan Stewart, who told me just to forget the visit had ever happened. Sure enough, nothing ever came of it, and I never did get a new grist bin.

Charles Grant-Gordon regarded Girvan as his own personal fiefdom; he even had an ocean-going yacht which he kept in Girvan harbour and which had to be brought ashore each winter by the distillery men because it was kept at the distillery. When Charles wanted the yacht brought in, everything came to a halt. It was a massive thing, and it needed all available hands to deal with it. Come the spring, the whole process happened in reverse. Needless to say some of the distillery staff were put to good use during the winter with repairs and maintenance work on the vessel.

The company had an old farmhouse up at the Cabrach, to the south of Dufftown, which was a famous area for illicit distilling in the 19th century. We had to make sure that it was prepared for the occasions when Charles and his family came to stay there . One day, I remember him coming down to the distillery and kicking up hell with Duncan Stewart because there wasn't enough sugar in the place! Things like that were the downside of the family company approach, but he was the only difficult one; everyone else was fine to deal with. Apart from himself and brother Sandy, the rest of the board was made up of non-family members, although the chairman, Eric Roberts, was their uncle by marriage. He had been brought in as a steadying influence when Charles and Sandy were too young to take over the company; he was a terribly pleasant man. There is still significant family involvement in the company today.

In October 1969 a good friend of mine, Jim Macmorran, who worked for SMD, invited me to the Highland Watsonian Club annual dinner in Inverness one evening. There I met Duncan McGregor, who, like Jim and I, had gone to George Watson's College in Edinburgh, and we all got talking. Over a few drams he asked me what I was doing, and he told me he had once worked for William Grant's too. A couple of months later I noticed an advert in the *Brewers' Guardian* for a manager for Tormore Distillery, near Grantown, and it said that the person to contact was Duncan McGregor, production director of Long John Distillers, who also worked as manager of Tormore. The plan was for him to be based at Tormore even after the new manager was appointed. He told me when we met to discuss the vacancy that he didn't think it would be a good idea for me to have the job! He had made a few enquiries about me and felt that because we were very similar in temperament there might be a clash of personalities if we were to work on the same site. So I gave up all thoughts of the Tormore job, and just carried on with my work at Balvenie, until in late January 1970 I got a phone call from Duncan inviting me to meet him at his home the following Saturday afternoon in order to discuss something of importance. He lived about a mile from Tormore Distillery and I drove there from Dufftown in very heavy snow. I was installed in a comfortable chair with a dram in front of the television, and we proceeded to watch the rugby international match between Scotland and Wales at Cardiff Arms Park which Duncan thought would interest me because there was a Watsonian playing scrum-half for Scotland, a chap called Graham Young, with whom I had been at school. But I couldn't see that his appearance in a Scotland jersey was that important to me. Scotland duly lost the match 9:3, after which Duncan suddenly turned to me and asked, 'How would you like to be manager of Laphroaig?'

'I've never thought about it,' I replied, adding tongue-in-cheek, 'Where is it?'

'You know fine well where it is', he said.

'Well, I'll have to think about it', I responded, 'You've hit me cold, and I've never even seen the place.'

'Look…do you or don't you want to be manager of Laphroaig?' he persisted. 'It's a heaven-sent opportunity.' I repeated that I needed time to think about it, and that I needed to know a lot more about the place and the job, but under his continued pressure I admitted that I was very interested. He took that as a yes, and arranged for me to go to Glasgow the following week to meet Long John's MD, Bill 'WL' Brown. I found an excuse to take a day off work at Balvenie, and the meeting with Duncan and Bill Brown duly took place.

I was offered £2,000 a year to move to Laphroaig, which was almost £500 more than I was being paid at Balvenie and I was also offered a company house and a car thrown in. I was well aware of the high profile of Laphroaig, and told them that I realised it was a great honour to go there as manager. I asked whether there was any chance of having the salary raised to £2,200, and was told that if I started on £2,000, they would review the situation after three months. On that basis I formally accepted.

It then seemed like a good idea to actually go and see the place with Kay, who, quite understandably, had misgivings about moving somewhere so remote. By this time it was late February, and a howling gale was blowing when we arrived at West Loch Tarbert to catch the ferry to Islay which was then the Western Ferries' vessel *Sound of Jura*. Western Ferries had seen off the competition of MacBrayne's at that point, and they were the main carrier to and from Islay. I have never been good on boats, and a force nine gale ensured that on that particular crossing I was very bad. People were being sick everywhere, all over the fittings and fixtures, themselves and each other, and in the saloon you had to cling to the uprights simply to stay standing. I regretted visiting the Tarbert Hotel for a bracer before the journey, where I had rather foolishly drunk a couple of pints of lager. Kay had had two Laphroaigs, so that her breath would make the right impression when we arrived…if, indeed, we did arrive, on the other side.

We were only ten minutes down the loch when I became convinced that we must be out in open water; the spray was such that you couldn't see a thing and the boat was heaving around so much, the screw propellers were coming clear of the water, making the whole vessel shake like hell. Hell was an appropriate word for the experience, and I began bitterly to regret my decision to accept the job at Laphroaig, which condemned me to several years of this sort of misery. I took myself off to the loo, where I remained for the next two hours, most of which was spent on my hands and knees, with the vomit of many men lapping around me on the floor. I would have considered it a blessed relief if the boat had sunk, as my will to live ebbed away with the miles. I had abandoned Kay in the saloon, where she apparently clung to an upright and closed her eyes. Somehow she managed not to be sick. Perhaps it was the Laphroaig.

After what seemed like a very large portion of my life had passed by, we made landfall at Port Askaig, in the north of Islay, at which time Kay and I met up again. 'You look terrible,' she said, and honesty compelled me to return the compliment. We drove off the ferry onto the delights of dry land and Duncan McGregor, who was staying at the Port Askaig Hotel, stopped us by the quay. We were driving a pea-green Triumph Vitesse and he greeted us with the words, 'Christ, you look the same colour as your car! You'd better come in and have a dram.'

The very last thing I wanted was alcohol in any shape or form, but we politely joined Duncan and his wife for a couple of whiskies. The second last thing I wanted was to have to speak to anyone, but Kay and I managed an hour exchanging pleasantries with Duncan and Mrs McGregor, before we set off to drive the length of Islay to our hotel at the opposite end of the island in Port Ellen. Without doubt, this was the coldest hotel I had experienced in my whole life, and the dining room was in a basement area. The place had a sort of grotto theme to it, which meant that there was a real live waterfall right next to our table. After the sea crossing, I found the juxtaposition distinctly unfunny. The sight and sound of the water meant that I couldn't eat a thing, and we decided to give up and retire to bed. Gratefully, I switched on the electric blanket…it didn't work. I slept in my dressing gown, and Kay simply put her dressing gown on over the clothes she was wearing and climbed into bed. So far, Islay was an unqualified disaster.

Next morning, I got up, still feeling terrible, and pulled back the bedroom curtains to be greeted by the most perfect day. The wind had dropped, the sun was shining, and everything was transformed. Kay and I went for a walk before breakfast, and I even managed to look at the sea. Better than that, I even managed to eat breakfast. Duncan McGregor then came to the hotel and drove us down the Kildalton road along the southern shore to Laphroaig.

Although Long John Distillers had taken over Laphroaig in 1962, they had only bought 51 percent of the business from Mrs Wishart Campbell, who had been the redoubtable Bessie Williamson prior to her marriage. Bessie was something of a legend in the business as she had inherited Laphroaig from Ian Hunter on his death in 1954. She had gone there in 1933 as his temporary secretary and shorthand typist, and never left. She was very much the matriarch of Laphroaig, and what Long John desperately wanted to do was get their systems, their controls, and their administration procedures in place at Laphroaig to replace the old culture of 'we do it this way because we've always done it this way'. I found out that this was the prevailing attitude very soon after taking up my position there.

I was introduced to Bessie and to her long-time associate Tom Anderson, the brewer. The previous manager, Bill Scott, had already left Islay and hadn't been there long enough to impose Long John's operational methods. Between 1962 and 1968/69 when Bill Scott had been appointed they had continued with the old system of the brewer effectively running the place, so significant changes had only just begun. They wanted someone to go across and get a grip of the distillery, and start to do things the Long John way. On the day I visited, I could see that there was clearly a mountain to climb, and that I was going to have to win over the hearts and minds of the staff before

I could begin to do anything. The sort of approach that might have worked at Balvenie certainly wasn't going to work on a Hebridean island. Bessie and many of the staff had been there so long that they couldn't see the problems that existed, but Duncan McGregor and the rest of the Long John board knew they existed and needed to be sorted out.

The problems were really ones of attitude as much as anything, and the difficulty of getting the best out of people who were inherently different due to the fact that most of the staff were born-and-bred Ileachs, as the people of Islay are known, with very few incomers. They were lovely people, I liked them enormously, but they had the same sort of laid-back approach to life as you find in Neil Munro's tales of Para Handy. From a commercial point of view this was not particularly good, even if there were many aspects of their culture and attitude to life that were really to be envied. There was a prevailing view at Laphroaig that if something had been good enough in the past, then there was no reason for it to be altered, and there was a real resistance to change of any sort.

However, one of the great attractions of going to Laphroaig was, as Duncan McGregor put it, 'You'll be king of your own domain. There's two or three hundred acres, and you can go walking or shooting, or you can take an afternoon off and play golf when you want.' It all sounded wonderful to me, though it wasn't actually to work out like that in practice. Another attraction was that the manager's house was an almost brand new architect-designed bungalow which had been built in the distillery garden; the setting was magnificent, with views out over Laphroaig Bay and the Irish Sea to the County Antrim coastline of Northern Ireland.

Putting that horrendous ferry crossing behind me, I began to feel that this could be quite a good move after all. There were the challenges of running a world-famous distillery, a decent salary, the opportunity to make a lovely home, and the allure of the promised company car, a Mark I Austin Maxi. It didn't seem to matter that there wasn't really very far you could drive it on Islay!

I took over as manager of Laphroaig at the end of April 1970, when I was still only 28 years old, and I felt that it was a real honour to be given this position at such a prestigious distillery when I was still so young. After my initial misgivings about going to live in such a remote location, I found that the island became a real part of me eventually, and even to this day I've never actually let go of it, because it had such a profound effect on my life. Once I moved on from Laphroaig, I got to go back to Islay on a regular basis in my role as general manager for Long John, and I've visited it many times since.

The challenges of Laphroaig included the need to produce more whisky from the distillery, and to improve water management. This had been slack, to put it politely, and they had frequently run out of water, despite a high level of rainfall. The yields were very poor too. When I left Balvenie they were around 2.9 proof gpb, and Laphroaig was only managing 2.56. The distillery was also extremely untidy, and 'housekeeping' was non-existent. I realised that in taking on the job I could have fun trying to meet all the challenges, and there looked to be many, and do myself some good in terms of my future career in the process.

Kay was pretty quiet during the visit to Islay. No doubt she didn't like the prospect of leaving her teaching job in Dufftown, where she had settled well, and her family in Elgin. I think she was wondering what she was going to do on the island to fill in her time. She had quite a lot of misgivings, and wasn't sure how she was going to be able to cope with the isolation. On the positive side, she liked the house and the garden. She did, however, consider staying on the mainland, while I lived at Laphroaig, but Long John were not impressed with that idea, as what they wanted at Laphroaig was stability. Eventually, Kay was won over, and we went to Islay together.

When I told Grants I was leaving, they asked me on a number

of occasions if I would reconsider, and said they thought I had a great future with the company. We parted on very amicable terms, however, and whenever I came across any of the Grant's people in years to come they were always extremely friendly towards me. I don't think I would have been offered, or felt I could have accepted, the Laphroaig job if I hadn't left the 'nannying' culture of DCL and joined Grants, and my time at Balvenie had certainly not been wasted.

However, before the great adventure at Laphroaig could begin, there was the small matter of getting our furniture out of the house at Balvenie, but this time at least it didn't rain, and, mindful of the railway bridge, we got a removal van to approach Dufftown from the other side of town!

Chapter 5
Islay:
Finding Our Feet

We made the crossing to Islay at the end of April 1970 and arrived with all our belongings at our new house at Laphroaig, which had been spruced up since our previous visit to Kay's precise specifications. Or rather, it had been repainted. This was the work of Archibald Macdougall, known to the entire island as 'Baldy', and the man whose company had built the house in the first place. The house was very well built, but when it came to Baldy's interpretation of our colour scheme there had definitely been a breakdown in communication. Either that or 'fawn' only came in the guise of 'banana' on Islay. Similarly 'white' was 'magnolia', and so it went on through every room of the house. I can't say this unduly distressed me, but it was clearly important to Kay. As there was no school teaching job available for her, she was going to be the one spending most time in the house, and her concern was understandable.

Matters were not improved by the necessity of having to fit our Balvenie curtains and carpets into the new house for reasons of economy. That would probably not have been a problem had a carpet fitter been available at short notice, but on Islay there wasn't one. This was a first taste of how island life could differ from the mainland in terms of supposedly minor matters. There was only one thing for it, I would have to attempt to lay the carpets myself. The main entrance hall and passages were finished in parquet flooring, so those areas could happily be ignored, and the kitchen was fitted with orange vinyl floor tiles, which did nothing to flatter the banana-coloured walls, but at least it meant I could leave the room well alone. I set to and began to tackle the lounge and after a lot of sweating, swearing and pulled back muscles I ended up with a floor fully covered with carpet…or rather many pieces of carpet which lay side by side and were secured with an embarrassingly prolific number of floor tacks.

When the sun shone into the room or a light was switched on they all appeared to wink at you, and after a few days we could bear it no more, and began to position pieces of furniture strategically over the largest concentrations of metal heads. All in all, this seemed to me a job pretty well done, but when I suggested expanding my carpet-laying talents to the bedrooms, Kay was firm in her refusal, and eventually we got Fraser MacArthur of the local furniture store in Port Ellen to deal with them. In addition to running the furniture business, Fraser was also the local photographer for weddings, ceilidhs, anniversaries and the like. He was a busy man, and we soon learnt that patience was a real virtue on an island like Islay. It was, after all, a Hebridean who said, 'When God made time, he made plenty of it.'

The first evening we were in the house Kay ran a bath and shouted to me that the water must be contaminated with something as it was dark brown in colour. She refused to get into the water, which to me looked as though it had run straight off the hill, through the peat bog and into our water tank. This, it turned out, was exactly what it had done. Our drinking water was the same. Another lesson about life on Islay.

In addition to Kay and myself, our household also consisted of our dog Kim, which we had had since Dailuaine. She was a cross between a retriever and a springer spaniel bitch and she looked like a black and white retriever. She was very lovable, but an extremely silly dog, which was hardly surprising considering her parentage. A few months later the family was enlarged when Kay and I adopted our son, Jonathan, having tried for some time to start a family of our own. I also, of course, now had my first company car, a Mark I Austin Maxi. The Maxi was not the most blistering of performers, but then that wasn't much of a factor on Islay, and it was equipped with a gearbox that made shifting feel like moving a rod between rubber bands in a bed of chewing gum. But at least I had a company car, and I grew quite attached to it.

The distillery of Laphroaig essentially consisted of a series of ramshackle old stone buildings, which had been lime-washed many times over the years. The main buildings were situated on the shoreline by the Bay of Proaig, or as Laphroaig translates from the Gaelic, 'The Place in the Hollow.' The Bay of Proaig is a small inlet which separates the shore from the open sea by means of a headland and an outcrop of greenstone rocks. In days gone by, the coastal steamers, or 'puffers' as they were known, used to come into the bay and empty their cargo of coal into barges pulled by rowing boats. Horses and carts would then wade out into the water to meet them. The contents of the barges were then emptied into the carts, and subsequently taken up to the distillery. By my arrival on the island this practice had long since ended, with coal being brought in by ferry to Port Ellen, and the bay was primarily used as the discharge outlet for distillery effluent.

Seen from the sea, the buildings of Laphroaig from right to left were warehouses, the office block, malt barns, the kiln, the mash house and the dried grains production plant. The walls of these buildings were subjected to a very severe buffeting by the Atlantic gales during the winter, and at other times when there were high seas. In addition to the ranges of old stone buildings there were some fairly temporary-looking structures sheltering behind them. The main one was the stillhouse, which had been relocated from its original home next to the mash house into what had formerly been the coal shed. This had occurred when the distillery had been converted from burning coal in the boilers and stills around 1967, to using an oil-fired boiler and steam-heated stills. The ex-coal shed was a rather sorry affair, partly roofed with corrugated iron, while the rest was covered with asbestos slates. These used to leave the roof with monotonous regularity every time there was a gale, and it was frequently necessary to wear a waterproof coat when working in the stillhouse.

If you were entering or leaving Port Ellen by the ferry, the whole shoreline along the water between Islay and the little island of Texa was fascinating because it was studded with whitewashed distilleries. Texa had once been owned by Laphroaig Distillery, and now belonged to Bessie Campbell. It was renowned for its goats which had interbred for generations and were the strangest looking creatures you ever laid eyes on. As you sailed round the corner out of Port Ellen the first thing you saw was the group of buildings which made up Laphroaig, followed by Lagavulin, and a mile further on, Ardbeg. Each of these three distilleries produced very distinctive whiskies, all quite different in character, yet all unmistakably Islays. It was fascinating to me to think that the distilleries could be in such close proximity to each other, yet produce such different whiskies. Islay was a small island, yet it had eight working distilleries at that time, each producing an entirely different whisky.

Laphroaig had been established in 1815 by the Johnston family, and when I was there the name of the company was still D Johnston & Co (Laphroaig) Ltd. As such, the chairman of the company was Bessie Campbell; the distillery having been sold to Long John by Bessie on an instalment basis, the total price being around £300,000. That was a lot of money to pay for a business in those days, especially considering that the entire profit of Long John International was around £900,000 in 1970. Bessie was still very much the figurehead of Laphroaig when I went there, and was greatly loved by the staff and the local community. Laphroaig had become known locally as Islay's second Labour Exchange because Bessie could not listen to a hard-luck story without giving in and providing a job for the person concerned, even though there was usually no job at all. Eventually this became a problem for the new owners, and therefore for me, as I was the man who had to deal with it. Bessie spent most of her time after I arrived filling hampers with her books and memorabilia, as it was her aim to cut her ties with Laphroaig once Long John had assumed a particular percentage of the shareholding.

The Laphroaig staff at that time consisted of many family groups. The senior clerkess was Rachel McAffer – a very common Islay surname – and she had been at the distillery for all her working life. She was extremely good at her job, but somehow also found time to run a croft up beyond Lagavulin and a guesthouse in Port Ellen! Her 'junior' was Betty McAffer, her niece, who had also worked at Laphroaig since leaving school. The brewer, who had additionally served as previous manager, was Tom Anderson, who had gone to Laphroaig in the late thirties after working on the land near Edinburgh, so he and Bessie went back a very long way. One of the labourers was an Oban man by the name of Hamish Campbell, and he was married to Tom's daughter Betty.

The head warehouseman was Ian Maclean, one of three brothers who worked at the distillery. The others were Hector, a stillman, and Duncan, who was also a warehouseman and the Land-Rover driver. Ian was a tall, upright man who even to this day, I believe, cycles everywhere, despite being about 80 years of age. Ian was known as 'The Stag', on account of his being a very tall, imposing man who loped rather than walked, Hector was 'The Fox' because he was small and red of hair and complexion, while Duncan was always 'The Guttie', because he had a permanently bad stomach. John McNeil was the Laphroaig gardener, whose precious vegetable plot had been destroyed to make way for the manager's house, which was named in

Gaelic *Tigh an Garadh* – the House in the Garden. John doubled as the hairdresser, working from his salon in the greenhouse. His two sons also worked at the distillery.

It was, therefore, necessary to be very careful what you said about anyone, as they were usually related to the person you were talking to, and if not, word still pretty soon got back to a member of the family, especially as most of these people lived in Laphroaig Distillery village!

Another Laphroaig worthy was James MacFarlane who worked in the cooperage, preparing the empty casks for filling. He was known as 'Posh'. This nickname came from the fact that he suffered from adenoids, which was apparently enough to make him sound distinguished among his fellow workers. He was registered disabled, and walked with a stick as a result of what he claimed was a war wound. On Friday evenings at five o'clock, however, he could almost sprint from the Land-Rover into the Ardview Hotel in Port Ellen for his first drink of the night! Whenever there was a particularly difficult or dirty job to do, James would always ask adenoidally, 'Is there a dwab★ for it?'

Dick Swarbrick was the excise officer at Laphroaig, and like many excisemen he didn't much like having to work a five-day week and be tied down to when he would be in any particular place. When there was any non-routine work to be done at the distillery which legally required an excise presence, we had to give the officer advance notice in writing. On one occasion I let Dick Swarbrick know that we were going to have some warehouse windows blocked up to comply with fire regulations, and that he needed to be there while the work was done. Come the morning in question, the builders arrived but there was no sign of Dick. Eventually I let the men go ahead and do the work without an excise officer, and when he subsequently found out, Dick went berserk down the phone at me, threatening me with all sorts of retribution for breaking regulations. He was a Lancastrian, from Bolton,

★dram

and he had a terrible temper. I pointed out that I had supplied him with advance written notice, and the fault was his. It turned out he had spent the day fishing on Loch Gorm! That evening, he turned up with a fresh trout as a peace offering! Generally, we got on well.

If I had enjoyed little contact with other distillery managers during my time in Dufftown, the situation was very much the opposite on Islay. I rapidly became aware of who my opposite numbers were in the island's other distilleries. The manager of Ardbeg was Hamish Scott, while at the neighbouring distillery of Lagavulin it was Jack Wilson. Port Ellen Distillery was still working in those days, and was managed by Angus Mactaggart. DCL owned Lagavulin, Port Ellen and also Caol Ila, in the north of the island, with Caol Ila being managed by Evan Cattanach. DCL was the largest distillery owner and employer in the island. They had a resident distillery inspector on Islay, who also visited the warehousing complex at the long-defunct Hazelburn Distillery in Campbeltown. Rather than build lots of new warehousing on Islay, DCL shipped surplus spirit from its Islay plants to Hazelburn, where it could mature in maritime conditions very similar to those on Islay, thus maintaining consistency.

When I was on Islay, the inspector was George Ballingall, who was also an Old Watsonian. The manager of Bowmore Distillery, the oldest on the island, dating from 1779, was Alistair Ross, who had been a fellow trainee of mine. Gilbert Duncan was manager at Bunnahabhain, and Peter Logie ran Bruichladdich for Invergordon Distillers. He subsequently became the first manager of the new Auchroisk Distillery on Speyside. (Bruichladdich is now, sadly, mothballed.) The various managers met up from time to time in order to help each other out when someone had, for example, a technical problem, and there was a sense of comradeship irrespective of company rivalry on the island. We would also, of course, meet up quite regularly at social gatherings.

Chapter 6
Islay:
Ringing the Changes

When I took over at Laphroaig, the spirit yields were as low as 2.54 proof gpb, which was just not acceptable, and something had to be done quickly to improve efficiency. Among a number of changes, we introduced better cleaning procedures to ensure that we could get efficient fermentation to improve the amount of alcohol produced at that stage in the production process.

One of the difficulties of using heavily peated malt is that it can create quite inefficient fermentation, due to its high phenol content. Laphroaig's malt phenol content was exceptionally high, around 35ppm, so one could not realistically compare the malt and its potential efficiency with that produced, for example, in central Speyside, where malts tended to be lightly-peated. The Laphroaig process water flowed out of a peat bog, the water used to steep the barley in our maltings came out of a peat bog, and we then used mounds and mounds of furnace peat in the kilns to increase the phenol levels even more, so it was no great surprise that our yields were lower than at many mainland distilleries. It took me some time to appreciate this really, and I remember the brewer Tom Anderson saying to me one day, 'You can't get good yields like you're wanting because of the high level of the peat, do you not understand? It's the quality of the peat, low sulphur peat, that gives us the smokiness, otherwise you don't have the Laphroaig.'

We were dealing with old methods and old plant, because there had been very little investment in the distillery for a long time. It certainly wasn't hi-tec, in fact I would say it wasn't even lo-tec, more no-tec at all, but it did have the magical ingredient of the personal touch – the fact that the employees were turning the malt, shovelling in the peat, making grist in a manually-set mill and all the rest. This made our attempts to increase yields seem a very personal thing to the men, who felt that we were trying to take away the individuality of Laphroaig from the people who lived there, who drank, ate and slept Laphroaig.

As the yields increased, however, so the men began to take a greater pride in their work and in the workplace itself. We undertook a considerable amount of landscaping work, removing a huge heap of rubble which occupied a lot of ground in front of the distillery office. This, I discovered, had been Laphroaig House, where the owners of the distillery had formerly lived, and when it had been demolished a year previously, the remains were just left where they fell. We cleaned all this up, and brought in topsoil to landscape the area. We also improved the distillery yard, which was just like a farm track, by clearing it and laying tarmacadam. Additionally, we built a large loading bay so that when the new filling store was operating we could roll the casks out of it and straight on to the distillery lorry.

What you might call the 'housekeeping' of the distillery had been terrible when I arrived, but now the men were sweeping the yard and polishing the stills, and we put an annual painting programme into effect. Everything was still manually controlled, of course, but the staff had more interesting jobs at that time than they subsequently did after automation. Some of them confessed to me years later when I met them that they were bored to tears just pressing buttons, and had been much happier when the job had required the use of hands-on skills.

The ultimate owner of Laphroaig and Long John Distillers was the Schenley Corporation of Cincinnati, and soon after my arrival at Laphroaig we were visited by two representatives from the company, Bart Crowley and Al Owen. They were from the engineering section of the corporation, and were on the island because the results from Laphroaig were lower than had been expected that year. Also significant was the fact that the parent company was owned by an entrepreneur who had interests in other drinks-related businesses in the USA, along with supermarkets and even film studios. Some of these ventures were performing poorer than expected as well. Schenley, therefore, were on a cost-cutting mission and an efficiency drive to increase profits, so Crowley and Owen had been sent to Islay on a fact-finding mission to decide whether the company should keep Laphroaig, and if it was to do so, what could be done to improve productivity and cut costs.

This was obviously a tense time for Kay and I, as we had just uprooted ourselves to Islay, and we didn't know what the future held for Laphroaig. Eventually Schenley decided to keep Laphroaig, and budgets were agreed for all the company's Scottish distilleries, though it was not easy to stick to a strict budget on an island like Islay, where all costs were at least 20 percent higher than on the mainland.

It was decided that if Laphroaig was to be kept, then its capacity should be doubled, and we undertook to produce whisky while all the developments were going on. We also tackled the problems of the low yields during the same period as we were planning the upgrading and capacity increase. It was vitally important that we were able to demonstrate to our American masters that yields were improving during 1970, and we did manage to increase the yield from 2.54 to 2.75, which was considered quite good, given the type of process and the style of heavily-peated malt that we were using. Attention to detail in the maltings was an important part of increasing the yields, and the men were paying more attention to the barley during malting, taking steps to slow it down where necessary and generally paying more attention than they had done in the past, and this certainly helped.

One of the first improvements we made was to put in a new fire ring main system, and we decided to use it to run sea water through old condensers, which were shipped to the island from the Strathclyde grain distillery in Glasgow. This helped to increase the supply of process water in the short-term, but the sea water damaged the copper piping inside the condensers, and we eventually installed a cooling tower and built a dam behind the stillhouse. We recycled the water from the stillhouse condensers through the cooling tower and reused it along with fresh water. This helped to increase the production capabilities of the distillery from 360,000 proof gallons per year to around 430,000 proof gallons per annum. This was not nearly enough, however, and the decision was taken to increase the tun room and stillhouse capacities, with the aim of increasing the overall capacity of the distillery from 430,000 gallons per year to more than 700,000 gallons.

We also had to look at the water supply very carefully, because it was well known that Laphroaig frequently ran out of water. This was just due to poor water management, as the distillery was served by a somewhat distant hill loch, Loch na Beinne Brice. In order to conserve water it was necessary to go up there regularly with a dip rod, and adjust the outlet valve accordingly. Prior to Long John taking over Laphroaig, what had happened was that when water got scarce, someone had simply gone up to the loch, opened the valve, and let the water run until the loch was empty.

One day I went up to Bowmore in the Land-Rover with 'The Guttie', and on the way he pointed out to me the remains of an old bridge which had been washed away in a flood before the Second World War. He said to me, 'There used to be plenty of water on this island, but there was a shortage after the war, until Long John took over, and since then we have had nothing but rain.' The reality was that the distillery hadn't run out of water since Long John took over due to better water management – it was nothing to do with changes in the climate! As part of the improvements, we built a new dam at Kilbride, capable of holding five million gallons of water.

The maltings were also uprated to cope with five or six kilns of malt a week as opposed to the normal three; we did this by putting oil-fired burners into the kilns. This reduced the drying time from 48 hours to around 30 hours, which meant we could take off six kilns one week and five the next. As a result of the projected increase in capacity at Laphroaig, we had to enlarge the cask filling store, and we upgraded an old farm building, putting in a new vat room with a new spirit receiver. Previously spirit receivers at Laphroaig had always been wooden, but this one was stainless steel. We then needed a larger reception area for empty casks and a larger area for the new automatic filling gun. We also needed, of course, to increase our warehouse storage capacity. All Laphroaig which is bottled and sold as single malt is matured on the island so we had to build a new warehouse which could hold half-a-million proof gallons of spirit if required. An extra block was later added, giving a total capacity of one million gallons. Baldy Macdougall, the builder of our house, got the contract to erect the warehouses; in fact, he worked for various distilleries on the island. Fortunately for Laphroaig, the panels for the new structure came pre-painted.

To increase the capacity of the tun room we built three new double-size Corten steel washbacks. Personally, I would have preferred to see pine washbacks of the sort previously used in the Laphroaig tun room for more than a hundred years, but the steel ones were introduced because they were considerably cheaper. By this time Schenley was clearly dictating terms to the Long John engineering department, which was rapidly being expanded, rather to the alarm of we distillers, who may not have been engineers, but who did understand how distilleries functioned and how to make whisky. We felt that the engineers were taking control, and our positions were, to some extent, under threat.

When it came to increasing the capacity of the stillhouse at Laphroaig in 1972 there was quite a confrontation, because the engineers and the distillers came to the situation with views which were poles apart. Increasing the number of wash stills was comparatively simple, because there were already two, and the installation of one extra wash still could take care of the extra capacity required. When it came to the spirit stills, however, two new ones were needed, but on grounds of cost-effectiveness it was decided that one double-sized still would be installed. It was to be the same in every respect as the three small existing spirit stills, but it was to be twice as large. The engineers and the bosses of Schenley were warned that to do this would inevitably change the character and the style of Laphroaig from its traditional heavy, peaty, oily, smokey, phenolic, iodine-like form. Unfortunately, in my opinion and that of most people who knew the 'old' Laphroaig, the spirit did change. From the point of view of the traditionalist, what emerged was not the Laphroaig of old, though, in purely commercial terms, the production of a lighter Laphroaig may have been for the better in the long run, giving the whisky a wider following.

At the end of the day, I would have to say that economic considerations mattered more than maintaining the quality and tradition of one of Scotland's finest and most distinctive whiskies. Nevertheless, I was proud to be the manager of Laphroaig, and to have played my part in the expansion, at least up to the point where the new spirit still was installed. We had all put in an immense amount of time and effort in order to implement the changes, and whatever reservations one might have had, we helped ensure the survival of the distillery as part of Long John International and helped it to have a bright future. Duncan McGregor's observation that I would be king of my own domain and in a position to play a round of golf whenever I felt like it had, however, proved rather wide of the mark!

Many more changes were implemented after my time at Laphroaig, aimed at automating the plant, and I don't think they were for the better. It's still a lovely location, the people working there are still great people, but I feel the distillery has lost a lot of its character.

It seems very unfortunate that decision-makers who set foot on the island maybe once or twice a year seek to impose change on a culture that inherently doesn't want this change. It is within the power of the workforce to make a success or otherwise of any particular operation on an island where life can be very isolated. This is often not appreciated by the decision-makers, sitting in their plush offices in Glasgow, Cincinnati, Montreal or wherever else the far-flung seats of distilling power happen to be, and it often seems to me that they could have got far more out of their staff if they had approached matters in a more sensitive way, and appreciated the culture of the people with whom they were dealing. Progress can, after all, sometimes be a regressive step, especially on a Hebridean island where many aspects of life can be so different from the mainland. You could never imagine what island life was really like, unless you had lived there and been invited into the community and its social life as myself and my family were by the people of Islay. You couldn't have met friendlier, more humorous folk, and they were also very resourceful, which was a result of living on an island which could be cut off from the outside world for days on end when the weather was too bad for the ferries to sail or for the daily BEA Viscount air service from Glasgow to fly. The Ileachs were a phlegmatic people, who would have to remind me from time to time, 'Well if it doesn't happen today, then it will happen tomorrow. And if not tomorrow there's always the day after. When the Man himself made time, Mr McDougall, he made plenty of it.' After a time I came to realise that however inconvenient it might be from the point of view of the business of distilling if ferries didn't sail and supplies didn't arrive, there wasn't anything I could do about it, and I learned to accept it. Well, as much as a non-Hebridean ever could, at any rate.

While we were in the process of expanding Laphroaig, Edward Heath's government was experiencing many difficulties, with the miners' strike and the Middle East oil embargo which gave the feeling that we were all about to return to the Middle Ages, while living in the second half of the 20th century. The disruption to our everyday life, although pronounced, was not nearly so difficult to cope with on an island like Islay as it was on the mainland. The Ileachs had long been used to disruption of power supplies, and hardships such as damage by gales and floods, so they tended to take the problems of the early seventies in their stride. Sometimes it even provided good excuses to have a party.

At Christmas in 1971 the nation was preparing dinner intermittently by cooking as and when power was available. There was no gas supply on Islay, except in bottled form, and in fact the arrival of mains electricity was a comparatively recent event, coming by way of a pipe which had been laid from the mainland to the island of Jura, and then under the Sound of Islay. The power supply tended to fail from time to time and when that happened, the old electricity generating station on the outskirts of Bowmore was brought back into use. Bowmore is noted not only for having the oldest distillery on Islay, but also for its round church, which stands on the hill overlooking the township, its distillery and Lochindaal. Legend has it that the church was built in the round so that evil spirits had no corners in which to hide, but plenty of spirits, whether considered evil or benign, found their way into the church inside the congregation!

Because of the crisis of fuel supplies affecting the nation, a state of emergency was declared; it was signed by the Queen in front of me at Laphroaig. To be strictly accurate, it was signed on board the Royal

Yacht *Britannia*, which was anchored just outside Port Ellen harbour, in full view of my office window. In those days, the Queen undertook an annual round-Britain cruise, which finished in Aberdeen so that she could then go to Balmoral for her Scottish holiday. The declaration was presented to her by Robert Carr, the Home Secretary, as *Britannia* was passing Islay.

Due to the electricity supply difficulties caused by the miners' strike and the inability of the old Bowmore generator to cope effectively when the mains power suffered one of its not infrequent malfunctions, Long John decided to install generators at Laphroaig and Tormore on Speyside. The Hydro Board had proved unable to generate continuous supplies of electricity to Tormore during times of industrial calm, never mind during periods of industrial unrest!

The Laphroaig generator was installed in the autumn of 1971, so when power supplies were cut off we continued to distil, which proved a wonderful morale-booster to our staff, who were used to being the poor relations of the Islay distilling community, because so little investment had gone into the plant before Long John took over. They could boast in the pubs that their distillery was still working at full capacity when others were silent, and that their manager knew how to keep things going in difficult times.

Although an apparently minor matter, this actually proved quite a turning point in winning over the 'hearts and minds' of most of the workforce, who, not unreasonably, had proved quite resistant to change. They saw, probably for the first time, that their working futures might be brighter, without them having to alter their ways of working too dramatically. I had also made a point of consulting them about all the changes we were making along the way, so that they felt part of the decision-making process. Eventually, they came to enjoy being associated with what was at that time Islay's most modern distillery.

By Christmas 1971 I was beginning to feel good about the way life was going at Laphroaig, and Kay's parents came over from

Elgin to Islay for the first time to spend the festive season with us. They flew into Islay around lunchtime on Christmas Eve and were taken to Tigh na Garadh, while I was busy fulfilling my Yuletide role as the bountiful manager dispensing drams to his workforce. At 2pm, the morning shift went off duty and so before leaving the distillery they turned up at the 'dramming table' in the recreation hall for their measure of 15-year-old Laphroaig. I, of course, joined them in a drink and wished them well for Christmas. At half past four, the day men finished work and the process was repeated, and the same thing happened again with the back-shift workers who were allowed to leave at around six o'clock as it was Christmas Eve. After my six o'clock dram I was feeling in pretty good order, for these were not 'bartender's measures' we were consuming. Far from it, these were 'gentlemen's measures'.

The garden of my house was situated about 50 yards from the recreation hall, and so after the final round of dramming I set off on the short journey home to Kay and the in-laws. As I made my way across the garden I was puzzled by the large pools of ice which had unaccountably formed during the afternoon, and which I duly smashed with my heels as I progressed towards the back door. Alerted by the sound of this activity, Kay and her parents were waiting by the door for me, and their welcome was not warm, though I'm sure I was smiling quite happily at them. It turned out that what I had very reasonably supposed to be sheets of ice were, in fact, a series of cold frames, the pride and joy of John McNeil, the gardener. Kay's father suggested rather brusquely that the best place for me would be my bed, and given the atmosphere, I was inclined to agree. My purgatory was not over yet, however. As I made my way through the kitchen Kay's mother fixed me with a stare and said, 'And I suppose this colour scheme was your idea?'

Matters were made worse by the fact that Hamish Campbell had accompanied me home from the distillery, and all this took place in front of him. Perhaps he didn't know that my home life wasn't always like this, or perhaps the effect of the drams meant that he didn't even notice. Hospitality dictated that Hamish be invited in, introduced to the merry company and given another dram, and then another. My father-in-law became better disposed towards me after a couple of drinks, and I think his initial reaction to my homecoming had been motivated by jealousy, as he had travelled from Elgin to Islay and then spent the afternoon with nothing stronger than tea to sustain him. I'm sure he'd expected me to arrive home and break open a bottle much sooner than I had, as he was very fond of a dram himself. After a time, Hamish's wife Betty appeared at our door asking for her husband, and said to him, 'Will you come out of there you great galoot and leave these good people alone.' Turning to Kay as she left she said quietly, 'I think perhaps it would be best if Mr McDougall didn't go out tonight.' Not much chance of that, I thought, even if my legs had been working properly. By this time my father-in-law was loudly singing *Granny's Hielan' Hame*, and I decided to act on all the good advice and head for bed.

Kay's parents left between Christmas and New Year, which was probably just as well considering the exertions of Hogmanay that lay before us. Kay and I decided to have a quiet Hogmanay dinner together at home, which we duly did with Jonathan tucked up in his bed. We saw New Year in quietly with a couple of drams of Laphroaig, but no sooner had we heard Big Ben chiming midnight on the telly than half a dozen of the distillery workers arrived to wish us Happy New Year. They came in, appropriated the record player and started to play 78's of Scottish dance music. Kay got out the shortbread and I opened a bottle of Laphroaig. The party had begun. By 3am Kay decided it was time for her bed, but we felt that I should go and first-foot the people in the distillery village.

There were 12 cottages and we only missed out one or two, which meant another ten generous drams on top of the dozen or so I had previously consumed. I finally ended up in a cottage in which the Mackinnon family lived. Norman Mackinnon was a maltman, and having previously been a plumber he had carried out a number of plumbing and heating-related improvements to his home. He insisted, in the deliberate way of one who had enjoyed some refreshment, in showing me in great detail the work he had done. This began around 5am, and continued for some three hours, when it was decided that breakfast would be a good idea. Norman's wife Fiona had cooked a chicken the previous day for New Year's Day lunch, but it was the only piece of food Norman was capable of locating by this stage of proceedings, so the four or five of us who were present began to dismember and devour the fowl. We were enjoying our slightly unorthodox breakfast when Fiona appeared in her nightie, slightly less than happy at the sight which greeted her. I offered her a dram to placate her, but for some reason this didn't seem to help, and I was asked to leave the premises, along with my fellow revellers. The way things were going, I'm surprised Norman wasn't asked to leave home! We then moved on to Hamish Campbell's house, where his wife Betty was prepared to take me up on my offer of a drink, and was quite happy for the party to resume there. The party continued all day, with Kay and Jonathan arriving to look for me in the middle of the afternoon, when her initial irritation was soothed with some Laphroaig. And so the party continued.

The festivities contrasted quite sharply with the very quiet Hogmanay we had spent at the end of our first year on Islay, when we were still comparative newcomers to Laphroaig. This time around we were known and accepted as part of the community, and nobody was interested in your background or the fact that you were the manager. Everyone was equal, and what mattered was camaraderie, and this aspect of island life was something we came to value very much. Incidentally, the story of the disappearing chicken did the rounds for a long time, and eventually entered Islay folklore. One of the great things about life on Islay was that you could be on first name terms with employees at ceilidhs and parties, yet at work you were always 'Mr McDougall'. This was not at my insistence, but was the way the staff themselves wanted it, and the relaxed informality of social occasions was never abused in the workplace.

One of the less popular moves I had to make was to reduce the Laphroaig workforce, as Bessie Campbell's policy of taking on anyone she felt sorry for had left us somewhat top-heavy in terms of labour. We cut back from 29 to 22, and eventually added another two again, to help cope with the increase in capacity. There was a lot of resentment at the cutbacks, not surprisingly, and some dark muttering that Mrs Campbell would never have done this, which, of course, was true enough. It really was a commercial necessity, however, and once the staff saw that their own futures were much brighter with all the changes being implemented, that the distillery's future was secure, their attitude began to soften.

Chapter 7
Islay:
Ceilidhs and Comrades

In the summer of 1972 I joined the Islay Sailing Club with my friend George Ballingall, Islay distilleries' inspector for DCL. George and his wife Winnie lived in a house at Port Ellen which had its own piece of beach, so he was able to run his boat up in front of the house and go sailing from there. Every Wednesday evening we sailed round to Port Ellen harbour and joined the other club members for a race. George was a man who saw himself as something of a country gent. Very much a plus-twos, huntin', fishin' and sailing man. He took the latter extremely seriously and didn't mince his words while at the rudder. On one occasion Winnie was sailing with us and she messed up a manoeuvre, bringing our boat to a dead stop while all our fellow competitors sailed past. George turned and shouted, 'Winifred, for God's sake will you move one of your arses.' She refused to speak for the rest of the evening and finally returned home for a dram to recover from being spoken to in such a manner on the high seas.

The sailing club contained lots of interesting characters, including Harold Hastie, who was the club's commodore, and also in charge of MacBrayne's ferry operations on the island. He was also co-director of Port Ellen lemonade factory! He was a leading light in the local amateur dramatic society, and as such, would usually be rehearsing a part whenever you met him or phoned, and he was a man who could make a two-minute conversation last for half an hour. One day he called an Extraordinary General Meeting of the club in MacBrayne's offices at the end of Port Ellen pier, in order to discuss whether the club should sell a boat it owned which was surplus to requirements. John McNab owned the general store in Port Ellen, where you could buy anything from a needle to an anchor, and he spent his Wednesday half-day afternoons in the White Hart. This was Wednesday evening, so he had enjoyed a fair drop of refreshment prior to the meeting. As Harold Hastie called the meeting to order there was the sound of a thunderous fart. Harold looked up from his desk, like a schoolmaster, and said, 'I would like to know who has just farted.'

There was silence.

'If I was a betting man,' he continued, 'I would put money on you McNab.'

'Aye, well, you see...' began John in response, before Harold cut him short by saying, 'That's a good enough admission for me. Gentlemen do we all agree that McNab has farted?' There was a chorus of 'ayes' around the room, and the business of disposing of the boat began. This took about two minutes, as a local farmer Andy Fraser offered the £140 asking price, and we all adjourned to the pub. Andy and his wife Janie eventually sold their farm and took the Port Charlotte Hotel, and they did well with it for a while, but Andy's idea that having a hotel gave him the perfect venue and excuse for a permanent party ultimately led to his going bankrupt.

The sailing club gave me a good opportunity to socialise with the locals of a Wednesday night, and our unofficial headquarters and drinking howf was the White Hart, owned by a club member by the name of Iain Wilson. Kay was not a great sailor, but she did used to enjoy the 'après-sail' in the White Hart with Winnie Ballingall, who became a great friend. When George and Winnie were recalled to

DCL's Elgin base in late 1972 Kay felt their absence quite keenly, particularly as we were living in a comparatively remote part of the island, and she didn't drive. DCL apparently felt that there was a danger of George 'going native' if he stayed on Islay much longer. Kay did, however, get a part-time job in the primary school in Port Ellen, where the schoolmaster was a real north-east man called Alec Collie, who came from Johnshaven on the coast near Montrose. In the best north-east tradition, he insisted on being called The Dominie. Alec loved shooting, and he was an excellent shot. Unfortunately, he would shoot anything that moved – pheasants, rabbits, blackcock…anything. Laphroaig had shooting rights over about 250 acres, right up to the boundary with Lagavulin Distillery. George Ballingall loved shooting too, and it was traditional that the manager of Laphroaig ran a Boxing Day shoot, although I actually hated shooting, and only went along with this because it was expected of me. I came up with a reciprocal arrangement with Jack Wilson of Lagavulin that we could follow pheasants onto each other's land when necessary. That was the sort of local agreement between distilleries that was so common on Islay, but which was not something I was used to back on the mainland. Alec Collie was invited along to the shoots, as was Iain Wilson of the White Hart, and over mince pies and several drams at our house after one shoot Iain said, 'I'm extremely pizzled as to why there are three pheasants in your bag and three in mine, when you are the host.' Kay heard this and burst out laughing and said, 'What do you mean you're pizzled, Iain?'

'What I mean', he replied, 'is that I'm puddled, er, no…I mean, er…I'm…umm…'

'Do you really mean you're pissed and you're puzzled?', she persisted. Looking relieved that an explanation had been arrived at, Iain said, 'Yeth', and promptly fell asleep.

The Collies left the island in 1973, which deprived Kay of more friends, but after her spell as a part-time teacher in Port Ellen, she set up a pre-school group for children of the distillery village at Laphroaig, which gave her contact with the distillery wives. We also set up a social club in the recreation hall at Laphroaig, resurrecting Ian Hunter's old full-size snooker table, which increased the camaraderie among the distillery workers.

One evening we had a dinner party at our house, and David and Joan Mottram who owned the Bowmore Hotel were invited, along with Andy and Janie Fraser. It was a very stormy Saturday night, and it was traditional on Islay that nobody arrived for dinner until after the pubs closed at ten o'clock! There was none of this mainland nonsense of 7.30 for 8.00; very often you would be sitting down to dinner at midnight. David Mottram had just taken delivery of a brand-new 3.5-litre Rover V8, of which he was very proud. For some reason, he was a great fan of Erwin Rommel, Hitler's Field-Marshal in North Africa during the war, and he would turn up in a leather coat, military cap, and goggles, pretending to be a tank commander.

By the time our guests left around three in the morning, the storm was at its height, with branches snapping off trees, and roof tiles flying everywhere, particularly, by the sound of it, off the Laphroaig stillhouse roof. What I didn't know was that the man who was working in the stillhouse that night had spotted we had company, and thinking that he wouldn't be detected, took off into Port Ellen for a drink or a woman or whatever, leaving the place unattended.

The tide was very high that evening, and a combination of that and the storm meant that the road to Port Ellen had flooded at a low point between Laphroaig and the village. Not long after leaving, therefore, all four of our guests turned up on our doorstep again. Unfortunately, David had driven straight into the flooded hollow, at which point the spanking new Rover's engine cut out, and the car began to fill up with sea water. David phoned the police to warn them the car was there, and after the car had been dragged out of the flood and pushed off the road the police gave our four guests a lift into Port

Ellen in order to knock up Iain Wilson at the White Hart so that they could stay there. By this time, the tide had receeded and the road was passable again, so I decided to go down to the White Hart in order to share a nightcap with everyone, as I was not officially on duty. On the way, we passed an abandoned Mini, which bore a striking resemblance to the stillman's car. It dawned on me what had happened; and I immediately turned back to the distillery, where I found the still room unattended. With the help of the mashman we kept the stills going until the day man came on at 6am.

The following morning I suspended the stillman from duty, and duly sacked him. But there was still another factor to consider; he was the shop steward at Laphroaig, at a time when the unions were getting powerful in the distilling industry, and he was in no mood to lie down. At that time the General and Municipal Workers' Union organiser for the distilling trades in Scotland was George Robertson, now Secretary of Defence and he was duly summoned by the stillman to fight his case. Robertson came over to Islay to see me and was an absolute gentleman. He was very professional and he obviously made it crystal clear to the stillman that if the union was to be of any use to the workers, then they, in turn, had to act responsibly, and that he could do nothing for him in this case.

The next shop steward at Laphroaig didn't fare much better, because one night when I made a surprise off-duty visit to the distillery, as I did from time to time, I went into the dark grains plant and found him sound asleep on bags of dried grains in the loft, while the drier was jammed from end to end with wet draff and the whole process ground to a halt. We then went through the same routine as before with me sacking the man, George Robertson catching the Islay ferry to meet me again, and once more leaving the island having found there was nothing he could do for his union member. We met occasionally over the years, usually on opposite sides of the table, as it were, but I was always impressed by George's professionalism and the fact that he was such a very pleasant man. (When I was appointed general manager for Long John in Glasgow some years later, totally out of the blue I received a charming letter of congratulation from George, by that time MP for Hamilton, and a rising star in the Labour Party.) Initially the dismissals didn't go down too well with the workforce, but I pointed out that negligence of that sort could jeopardise the whole operation, and was unfair on the vast majority of the staff who worked very diligently and responsibly.

●   ●   ●

We didn't often get snow on Islay, and when it fell it was something of a novelty. I only remember one snowy night on the island, and I wandered down into the distillery yard to check all was well, only to find Cally Smith, who worked in the dried grains plant, walking round in circles, and moving backwards and forwards in a very strange manner. I stood in the doorway of the malt barn to watch him, and soon realised that what he was doing was writing his name in the snow while peeing. Snow really was that much of a rarity on Islay. I crept up behind him and shouted 'Cally!' which resulted in him disappearing like a scalded cat towards his home without dotting the 'i'.

Cally was one of the older workers, about 60 at that time, and I remember him particularly in relation to a ceilidh we hosted one evening at Laphroaig. It was laid on for a party of 40 people who were to visit under the auspices of the SWA, and as the party included Earl Attlee we really pushed the boat out. In those days the whisky used on such occasions was all duty-free, along with Plymouth Gin and vodka which all came from Long John, while we bought in supplies of beer locally. We put on a great buffet and engaged the Mansfield Band, who played at most ceilidhs in the area, led by a man known as 'The Ferret', due to a remarkable resemblance to the animal.

Unfortunately, a force nine gale blew up during the day, and there were no flights or ferry sailings to Islay, which left the SWA party stranded in Tarbert and unable to include us in their itinerary. I duly phoned Long John head office in Glasgow to report this, and when I told them that I had invited all the island's distillery managers and their wives, the excise officers and their wives and all the distillery staff of Laphroaig, I was told to go ahead and have a really good evening. Not being one to disobey orders from head office if I could help it, we duly had one of the biggest and best ceilidhs ever held on Islay.

The gardener, John McNeil, ended up as he usually did on such occasions being carried out feet first, which meant that some of the haircuts he performed early the following morning in the greenhouse were less than perfect. Sometimes the hair was longer on one side than the other, occasionally there were bald patches that shouldn't have been there, but I always maintained that anyone who took the chance with John after he'd been refreshing himself in serious fashion the previous evening was very lucky not to lose an ear!

Cally Smith somehow managed to fall into the big whitewash bucket situated at the foot of the distillery office stairs. I found out about this the following morning when his wife came storming into my office, and told me it was all my fault.

'You have given him so much of the drink,' she started. 'I don't approve of the drink. Cally does not usually drink, as you know.' I knew nothing of the sort, in fact I knew very well that Cally would drink as much as he could get hold of, but I let that go. She continued.

'I'm not worried about Cally himself, in fact he can go to Hell, but he was wearing a new suit, and I would like the price of it.' I told her politely that neither myself nor Long John would be paying for the replacement of Cally's suit, as we had not forced the whisky down his throat.

'I think you should go home and discuss this with Cally,' I suggested, 'and by the way, did you know he writes his name in the snow when he's peeing?'

She was flabbergasted and left my office in high dudgeon, but the matter of the suit was never mentioned again.

Another fine ceilidh was held once at Bruichladdich Distillery, when the directors of Invergordon Distillers invited lots of us to join a reception being held for the SWA. Although it was a good ceilidh, the pre-function drink was probably more memorable. As usual, there were people from all the other distilleries on the island, including my friend Alistair Ross of Bowmore, and his boss James Howat, who came over to Islay for the occasion. A group of us went into the hotel at Bruichladdich for a dram before the ceilidh began, but the owners, a Mr and Mrs Paget, had fallen out in a rather serious way, and the husband had been locked out of the hotel by his wife. We found the door of the hotel locked, although this was the middle of Saturday evening, but Mrs Paget answered our calls, calmly explained the situation, and proceeded to serve us, having re-locked the hotel door once we were in the bar.

After a while we were joined by a couple of the Bruichladdich directors and various other 'high heid yins' of the distilling industry, along with a party of French VIPs who had been invited to the reception. As we were drinking and talking, the bay window at the front of the lounge bar was suddenly inched open and a bare leg appeared over the sill, followed by part of a kilt and then an arm. Before the rest of the person could enter, however, Mrs Paget ran across the room and slammed the heavy window shut, shouting as she did so, 'I've told you before and I'll not tell you again, bugger off!' There was a cry of pain like a wounded stag and a thud as Mr Paget landed in the shrubbery, then his wife calmly walked back to the bar and resumed serving.

In early 1972 Scotland were playing Wales at Murrayfield, and I decided to try to get to the match as it was a key game for the championship, and it was the era when Wales had one of its greatest sides, filled with players such as JPR Williams, Gerald Davies, Mervyn Davies, and Gareth Edwards. George Ballingall was also a keen rugby man, and he somehow managed to engineer a visit to DCL's Hazelburn warehouses at Campbeltown on the Friday, with the idea of perhaps going to Murrayfield the following day. I decided on the spur of the moment on Saturday to go to the airport and try to get a flight to Glasgow on that morning's Viscount. When I arrived at the airport I asked the BEA representative, Elizabeth McArthur, if there was any chance of a flight. This being Islay, she was not only a BEA receptionist, but also a hairdresser, and in fact I preferred to trust my hair to her than to John McNeil, whose hand-clippers were a particularly brutal instrument.

Elizabeth told me that there would not be a scheduled passenger service that morning as the plane was going to be used to transport a patient who had suffered a heart attack to hospital in Glasgow. Eventually, however, I was asked to step into the BEA boss's office, and once the ambulance appeared on the tarmac I was ushered onto the plane, and the doors were closed behind me. Apart from the heart patient, sectioned off behind a screen, I had the whole 70-seat Viscount to myself. Better still, we didn't land at Campbeltown as usual, and so I arrived in Glasgow sooner than I normally would have. I caught the train to Edinburgh and met George in Ryrie's pub at Haymarket, which was seething with Scots and Welsh fans. There I tried Old Cameron Brig grain whisky for the first time in my life, and I was so agreeably surprised, I tried several more. We went to the match which was a real see-saw affair. Scotland were winning until the last minutes of the game, when Gerald Davies scored in the corner for Wales, and then John Taylor made a seemingly impossible conversion from the touchline to give them victory by one point. The only way to deal with this setback was to take a few more Cameron Brig's in Ryrie's on the way to stay the night with my father and mother, who were by that time living in Edinburgh. The score line was galling, but we had seen one of the great rugby matches of all time.

Not long before that, George and I had been invited to watch the highlights of a Scotland match on television one Saturday evening by the local doctor, Archibald MacKinnon, known to the entire island as 'Doctor Archie.' The good doctor was very fond of a dram; so fond, in fact, that we all used to wonder how he managed to be up and working so efficiently and apparently clear-headed early each morning. The prospect of the visit was daunting, because Archie's idea of a dram was to literally fill a tumbler to the brim with whisky and then ask you if you took anything in it. Archie's peat basket sat beside the fire, and it must have contained the most volatile peat in Islay, as visitors used to empty their glasses surreptitiously into it as the evening wore on. The reason for our invitation was because Archie had the only colour television on the island, and this was my first experience of colour TV. He was a bachelor, and presumably well paid, and despite his drinks' bill he was one of the few people on Islay who could afford a colour set. Unfortunately, I never really got to see the game, as, true to form, Archie got us totally plastered before the highlights even started. Next morning, those of us who had 'watched' the match with Archie were dreadfully unwell, yet Archie was up and about as usual. Apparently, his secret was that he used to run himself a freezing cold bath the morning after every heavy night's drinking session, and leap in, right up to his neck.

Doctor Archie was among those present drinking in the Bowmore Hotel one evening prior to attending the official opening of the Bowmore Distillery visitor centre, organised by Alistair Ross for Morrison's, the distillery owners. As we were all drinking, the local police sergeant, Big Davie, came in and asked if Archie could attend a road accident with him. Archie was already to the beak by this time, and he announced to Davie, 'Aye, I'll drive.' 'No,' replied Davie, 'I don't think that would be for the best, but if you want to do something you can operate the blue light.' So they duly set off for the scene of the accident with Archie working the klaxon horn and the flashing light. Apparently he managed a competent stitching job, and was then brought back to Bowmore and the distillery ceilidh by Big Davie. Alistair Ross had booked Norrie Kimble And His Revolving Disco, and Norrie appeared in full cowboy rig, complete with Stetson and gun belt. The big hit at that time was a song called 'Jump Up and Down and Wave Your Knickers in the Air' and Doctor Archie was later seen trying to get Winnie Ballingall's knickers off in order to wave them in the air sometime around one o'clock in the morning. Winnie, needless to say, did not oblige.

Chapter 8
Islay:
Piety and Peat

One Friday afternoon I was phoned by the Church of Scotland minister in Port Ellen, the Reverend David Speed. The minister was dead against alcohol in any shape or form, which made his posting to Islay seem quite inexplicable to me. Whenever I met him he would say that people like me were causing lots of the world's problems, which was why he had so much work to do as the minister in Port Ellen. I have to say, I did have a degree of sympathy with him, because the church did not have such a hold on Islay as it did on some of the other Hebridean islands. I have to admit that I smiled broadly to myself, as he was asking me if I would show himself and the Moderator of the Church of Scotland around Laphroaig the following afternoon!

The moderator was the Very Reverend Dr Roy Sanderson, of the Sanderson's Vat 69 family, and while visiting Islay he not unnaturally wanted to tour one of the island's distilleries. 'We have our disagreements about such matters,' said the minister, 'but he's the boss.' I duly showed them around, and the moderator was clearly very knowledgeable about the industry, asking lots of intelligent questions, which helped make it an extremely enjoyable tour. When we got back to my office afterwards I asked the pair if either of them would like to join me in a dram. The minister declined, in fact he even declined to sit down, but the moderator was keen to have a drink. He actually had two, and we talked about distilling, religion, and lots of other matters. When he left he said, 'I think I've learnt more about life on Islay from you, Mr McDougall than I possibly could have if I hadn't come to Laphroaig.' Mr Speed and I never exchanged words again, and he was moved from Islay back to the mainland shortly afterwards. His attitude to drink did not go down well on the island, and as a result his church was never exactly full, except for funerals.

Funerals on Islay required great fortitude, but I had no idea what to expect when I attended my first one. Just about everybody went to a funeral on the island, and if you didn't then you were sure to offend someone. I was not prepared for the fact that an Islay funeral could last for up to four days. They had to hold burials to fit in with ferry times for mourners coming from the mainland, and they tended to have them much earlier in the day than I was used to. It was a mile and a half walk behind the hearse from Port Ellen to the graveyard, yet we were still back in the village by 10.30am. We had all been invited to the White Hart for what had been described to me as 'a bit of a reception'. This 'bit of a reception' boasted a master of ceremonies and a ceilidh band, and was a proper wake. After we'd all got a couple of drinks into us, the MC got up and said, 'Now for those of you who would like a refreshment, there is Lagavulin, there is Bruichladdich, there is Laphroaig. And for those of you who are teetoal there is the McEwan's Export and Tartan Special. Please enjoy the rest of the funeral because Hamish would have liked it that way.' I left around three o'clock the following morning, just as most people were warming up nicely. It was a way of life I had never experienced before, and I have never experienced since, and I found it quite difficult sometimes to keep my constitution in trim. Just about anything was a reason for having a ceilidh or a party.

There was a character called Sean O'Leary on Islay, who had

'dropped out' some years before, and he lived in a little caravan near Ardbeg Distillery. Sean was a big man with a huge red beard, and his mode of transport was a canoe built out of old oil drums, to which he had fitted a sail. We would often look out of the office windows at Laphroaig across the bay, and remark, 'Oh look, there's Sean going down to the pub.'

Sean was a very good artist, and he earned a living by painting things for people. He offered to paint Winnie Ballingall's children, but what she didn't realise was that once you had given Sean a commission you also had to keep him while he was working, and give him payments on account. Sean was a great pal of the Ardbeg manager, Hamish Scott, and he had painted what was known across Islay as the 'Ardbeg Muriel', featuring Hamish and the Ardbeg excise officer John Hopkin sitting down to a dram of Ardbeg from a cask. It was a wonderful piece of work. Right in the corner of the mural Sean had painted himself, looking through the window watching them.

When George Ballingall left Islay, the sailing club decided to have a farewell party for him in the Ardview Hotel in Port Ellen, and they asked Sean to make a speech, as he was a highly educated man who was very well read. He agreed to do so, but declined to come into the Ardview because he didn't have a suit. He always wore a kilt and wellington boots. He therefore made his speech through the pub window from the street, whilst being liberally supplied with drams. All we saw was a face and a big red beard at the window, but the speech was brilliant. I can't imagine that happening anywhere but on Islay!

They say that around a quarter of Islay is covered in peat, and if it is a physical characteristic of the island itself, it is also most certainly a characteristic of Islay whiskies such as Laphroaig. The distillery owned its own peat moss at Machrie, but one knock-on effect of all the expansion work was that we now needed twice as much peat, as we were making twice as much malt. In fact, we were soon burning 25 tons of peat per week at Laphroaig. Any new peat source had to possess exactly the same characteristics as that already in use, in order to maintain the continuity of the malt and therefore of the whisky itself, and I negotiated to purchase an extra 50 acres from the Machrie Hotel. We reckoned that with this we should be able to supply the distillery with peat for at least a hundred years at that time. It was important that the new peat land should be close to the existing one, because that way it should have had no higher a sulphur content than the old, and as you got closer to Bowmore along the part of the coast known as the 'Big Strand' you came into more sulphurous peat. Sulphurous peat can impart a flavour of sulphur right into the whisky in the bottle, and it gives the whisky a 'rubbery' nose.

We always hand-cut our peats at Laphroaig although we did try another method once. An automatic peat-cutter had been brought onto the island, but the peats it cut were too big and soggy, and never dried out properly; they weren't suitable for the natural-draught kilns at Laphroaig. We just didn't get the proper peat reek going through the malt when we used that peat so we decided to go back to hand-cutting our peat. But this too presented a problem because there were very few people capable of cutting peat in the quantity we required. We were needing to cut 1200 tons per year, which is a lot of peat to cut by hand. I was told about a number of local men who could do the job for us, but I was warned that they had a tendency to disappear into one of the Port Ellen pubs whenever the opportunity arose, or alternatively they would sit in the tin shed we had by the moss and drink their own supplies.

The principal cutters we took on were Hugh Carmichael, Alec Johnston and Tommy Johnston – known to one and all as 'The Twins', and Norman Campbell, whose alter ego was the cowboy DJ Norrie Kimble. Hugh Carmichael was called 'Huach', and Alec Johnston was 'Philco', though I never did discover why. Perhaps he could have been named after a well-known brand of pocket torch. He certainly lit up after a few drams, at any rate. I was still quite new to island life when we took them on, so I paid them something on account. This, of course, ensured that there was not a peat cut until they had spent it all! And so on each Friday afternoon the brewer and I ended up out on the moss with a chain – the old measure of 22 yards – calculating the amount of peat cut and the tonnage on the basis of peats per chain. We then had to take off a percentage for moisture, because the weight of the peat cut and the weight of peat delivered dry to the distillery differed dramatically. This was when the disputes began, with the cutters insisting we were deducting too much for moisture; sometimes they would even leave small spaces between the cut peats when they laid them out, so that they took up more ground when we measured them. By that stage, however, I was learning fast, and I wasn't going to be duped. We eventually came to an arrangement whereby if, for example, they had cut £100 worth of peat in a week, I gave them £50 at the end of the week, and then rolled up the remainder for them at the end of the cutting season. Given good weather, the season lasted from late March until early July, but you also needed to get all the cut peats into stooks to dry by the end of July. The drying didn't take long if the weather was reasonable, and we reckoned that all the peat would be delivered into the distillery by early September. Basically, it was a six-month operation and every year we put ourselves through the same scenario involving their money.

Towards the end of each season the lads asked what the running total was, and if there was any chance of another advance, which, of course, there was definitely not. They would then reply that they would do no more cutting, and that I would find no one else in the island who would do it for me. My response was always to assure them I would find somebody from somewhere on Islay and that unless they carried on with the job they wouldn't see the rest of their money. They would then resume cutting peat. Next there would be an argument over whether they would stook the stuff so that it could dry, followed by an argument over whether they would then load it onto tractor trailers to get it to the roadside, followed by an argument over whether they would then transfer it onto trucks and deliver it to the distillery. It was a ritual we had to go through every year, but we reckoned it was worth the trouble, because we did get the peat we wanted. They, in their turn, knew that they couldn't get decent money like that from anybody else.

The quality and consistency of peat was always important at Laphroaig and after the new, larger spirit still was installed when the whisky produced was somewhat lighter in character than before, it became even more vital. I knew that we could not compromise with the peat, and that it had to remain a trademark characteristic of Laphroaig. If we seemed to be digging our heels in and being traditionalists with regard to peat, it was for all the best commercial reasons.

We were then only making 30 percent of our own malt, the rest being made to our specification by commercial maltsters on the mainland and brought over by ferry. Now all the distilleries on Islay use malt from the huge UDV maltings plant at Port Ellen, which was built while I was on the island. Initially it was for the three DCL distilleries of Port Ellen, Caol Ila and Lagavulin. Until then the DCL had operated a puffer called the *Pibroch* which served their Islay distilleries with supplies of barley and malt, and took away casks of spirit, but the rest of the Islay distilleries relied on Western Ferries and the Tarbert haulier Mundell to transport supplies in and out. The little village of Bridgend is at the centre of Islay's road network, lying just north of Bowmore, more or less half way between the two ferry terminals of Port Askaig in the north and Port Ellen in the south, and at the point where the main road branches west to Bruichladdich and the Rhinns of Islay peninsula. As articulated lorries became larger, it was necessary to have the bridge across the road at Bridgend raised in height, and while all the non-DCL distilleries contributed to the cost, DCL refused to participate, because they had the *Pibroch* in service, and didn't see any advantage for them.

When DCL built the new maltings at Port Ellen, it gave the other Islay distillers some satisfaction to refuse to agree to suggestions that they might all use its malt. Obviously, this would have been economically more attractive for DCL, but the business about the bridge had not been forgotten even though the refusal to take Port Ellen malt was a false economy. Now, however, the hatchet has been buried, and the maltings serve all of the Islay distilleries.

●　　　●　　　●

An interesting diversion from life on Islay came in July 1971, when I was selected by Schenley to visit the USA. I was accompanied by Mike Walker, project manager of the new Strathclyde grain distillery in Glasgow, which was being built around the existing Strathclyde Distillery in the Gorbals. It was to be a very interesting and educational visit, and quite an eye-opener as to how they produced whiskey in the States and in Canada. The purpose of our trip was obviously to indoctrinate us with the spirit of Schenley, to help make us 'company men' and it was designed to be educational in all respects, both in practical terms and in personal development.

I had never been to the USA before, so it was all very exciting. We flew from Islay to Glasgow, then down to Heathrow, flying to the States the following morning. This was my first time in a jumbo jet, and I'd never seen anything so big in my life. I didn't believe that aircraft that large could stay up in the air, let alone fly at 30,000 feet! We flew into Logan International Airport in Boston, and caught a TWA DC9 to Cincinnati. All was well until the pilot began his approach to Cincinnati, only to pull out at the last moment. There was such a fierce electrical storm raging that he couldn't get down, and the plane climbed to around 20,000 feet, where it was again buffeted by the storm. It didn't do much for our morale to see the hostesses strapping themselves into their seats and putting their heads between their knees in case there was going to be an accident. I resolved never to complain about the Islay ferry crossing again and drank deeply of my gin and tonic.

The captain tried a second landing and had to abort again, after which he announced that we were diverting to Indianapolis, which was about 120 miles in the opposite direction to where we wanted to go. When we landed at Indianapolis there was another plane waiting to take us to Cincinnati, and we duly arrived in a fairly exhausted state at our hotel. Cincinnati was a town of about 300,000 people, which was quite small by American standards, but a big town to me.

One of the things that struck me most forcibly was the cheapness of everything compared to Britain. At that time the Albany Hotel in Bothwell Street in Glasgow was charging £50 per night for bed and breakfast, while our hotel in Cincinnati cost less than half that for far better facilities. Petrol, too, was less than half the price that it was in Britain, and the same went for housing, while salaries were certainly not half of those back home. The most wondrous thing for a man who had got used to life on Islay was the sheer number of television channels they had, and all of them in colour! They had more than 30 compared to our two.

Food came in very generous portions, as I discovered when I ordered a 'sandwich' for dinner, only to be faced with what was basically a French loaf capable of feeding at least four people. Our coffee cups were filled up by extremely attentive 'have-a-nice-day' waitresses without us having to ask. It was all very un-Scottish, and took a bit of getting used to, though I got to accept it during my stay. I was also introduced to iced tea, which was a totally new experience for me, and I drank quite a lot of it, for the humidity levels and the temperature in Ohio in summer were as alien to a Scotsman as someone saying, 'Have a nice day.'

Next morning we were collected by Jim Rulman, from the engineering section of Schenley. He had been assigned to look after us during our week's stay in Cincinnati. He and I were later to work together on the dam project at Laphroaig. We met Bart Crowley and Al Owen again at the enormous Schenley office complex, and were eventually taken to meet the big boss, Schenley's president, Ad Slone. Ad was short for Adolphe. We were shown into his suite and behind a massive desk in a massive air-conditioned room, smoking a massive Havana cigar sat the equally massive figure of Ad Slone. He was very charming and welcoming, and the atmosphere of the Schenley offices generally was laid back and friendly, not quite the high-powered, pressured image of corporate America that I had brought with me.

Jim Rulman took us out to look at the Ancient Age distillery, which had belonged to George Stagg and whose brand was IW Harper bourbon. The distillery is located in Frankfort, the state capital of Kentucky. Jack Lynch was the plant engineer, and he showed us around the distillery, which had its own bottling hall. There were trees all over the site, and at the end of our tour we were taken to the reception area, which was done out to look like a Wild West bar from a John Wayne movie. The barman slid a bottle of bourbon along the bar towards us, followed by a couple of glasses in best *True Grit* style. There was a full-scale cinema behind the bar, in which visitors were shown the company film; a forerunner of the audio-visual presentations which today are the norm in many of Scotland's distillery reception centres.

Our next visit was to Lawrenceburg Distillery, situated on the western outskirts of Cincinnati. It was a lovely distillery, very neat and tidy with quite a number of innovative features. For example, the warehouses were connected to the main production area, and also to the bottling plant by way of a railway system which made it seem as though casks were conveying themselves in batches of maybe a hundred at a time all over the site. The casks moved by gravity, with small inclines to slow them up in places. It was a remarkable system with an almost surreal feel to it – something I had never seen before and have never seen since.

Lawrenceburg had a tank room where the spirit was received; one peculiar tank had a glass top with an agitator inserted into the whiskey, a bit like an enormous Kenwood kitchen mixer. This was the result of an experiment by the former president of Schenley, Lew Rosenstiel, who thought that if he whisked the whiskey very hard he could make creamed whiskey! Not surprisingly it didn't work. The warehouses were beautifully clean and tiled, with constant temperature control, as were the bottling halls. Interestingly enough, most of the bottling hall operatives were men, whereas in Scotland they were almost exclusively women.

The day after our visit to Lawrenceburg, we went on a longer trip down to Louisville in Kentucky, the largest city in the state, close to the Ohio river. Here Schenley produced sour-mash bourbon. During the sour-mash process the residue of the previous distillate is held back and introduced to the fresh wort (coming from the mashing side of the following production run) in the open washback. This has the effect of giving a sourness to the wash, hence the name sour-mash bourbon. At this distillery I also saw open fermentation vessels for the first time, not manufactured out of wood or steel, but made of concrete, presumably because they could be built quickly and cheaply on site.

In addition to the distillery, we also visited the Louisville cooperage, which supplied almost all the casks used by the Long John company, because our policy was to use bourbon casks for our malts after they had been used for maturing bourbon. By law, bourbon casks can only be used once and so Long John could secure a ready supply of ex-bourbon casks for this purpose. Once the bourbon had been emptied out of them after four years they came back to the cooperage to be broken down into 'shooks', comprising their component parts of staves and ends, or shipped across as whole casks to the UK. The cooperage once employed a very young Cassius Clay, later Mohammed Ali, and, looking at the physiques of some of the men working there, I'm not entirely surprised it spawned a future heavyweight boxing champion of the world.

The countryside around Cincinnati and down into Kentucky was beautiful. Rolling hills, wide open spaces – the beginning of the Mid-West. The vastness of it all is what sticks in the memory. On the way to Louisville we went through Scott County, where the scale of some of the horse ranches had to be seen to be believed. My only previous experience of 'abroad' had been two trips to Europe, and those paled into insignificance beside the States, which made a huge impression on me.

From Cincinnati, we went on to visit the Schenley operation in Canada, in a place called Valley Field, which was about 30 miles north-west of Montreal. We were allowed by Schenley to fly first class to Canada via Chicago, and I remember thinking that the treatment offered to first-class passengers – with Moet champagne on tap – put into perspective my pleasure at having that flight from Islay to Glasgow all to myself.

At Montreal we were met by Jim McDougall, who drove us out to our hotel in Valley Field. Valley Field was, incidentally, the name of the manager's house at Tormore distillery, which had been built by Schenley in the late 1950s, and the two sites did have quite a lot in common physically, with the distilleries being situated amid large conifers at the foot of a range of mountains. Jim McDougall decided to take us to Valley Field's nightspot for dinner and entertainment; a place called the Balmoral, which boasted mock castle facades and a baronial hall where the meal was served. After dinner came the principal entertainment, which would certainly not have amused Queen Victoria, as it consisted of a performance by 'The Very Beautiful Jessica', who was a stripper. She was certainly far from ugly, and was a well-endowed girl but I fear that she was still an apprentice stripper at the time of our visit as she seemed to have serious difficulties in taking off her clothes. She couldn't get her top off over her head in one movement, it caught on her bra strap at the back, and suddenly her full breasts tumbled out, long before they were meant to be viewed by we punters. The Very Beautiful Jessica then ran off stage in floods of tears.

The distillery couldn't quite live up to the Balmoral, but it was interesting, nonetheless, and the whiskey it produced was Canadian rye. One unique thing about Valley Field was that almost all the staff spoke French, as it was in Quebec, which is quite unlike the rest of Canada in terms of culture. You wouldn't have known it unless someone told you, but the distillery was actually situated on an island in the St Lawrence river. Like all the other distilleries we visited across the Atlantic, Valley Field operated its own bottling plant on site, unlike Scotland where only Glenfiddich and Springbank bottled in this manner.

Back on Islay I found that my trip to the States proved helpful in as much as I had now met the men from Schenley's technical section in Cincinnati, with whom we were to work quite closely, and I obviously responded better to being told what to do by people I had met and with whom I was on first-name terms, rather than by faceless strangers.

●   ●   ●

In early 1974 I was asked to leave Islay and go to Tormore distillery, which had been the first brand-new malt distillery to be built in the Highlands this century. The first spirit had flowed there in 1959, and the distillery had officially been opened in October of the following year. Denis Nicol was the manager of Tormore, and Long John simply switched us over, with Denis moving to Laphroaig. Tormore was in need of some rejuvenation, and it was felt that I should be brought in to tackle this. The entire area of land which had been bought from the Seafield Estates extended to some 600 acres, bordering the A95 between Grantown-on-Spey and Aberlour-on-Spey and running right down to the River Spey. It included Tormore Farm, run by Vic Collier, who had been a tenant farmer first under Seafield Estates and latterly under Long John.

It was Schenley who really wished to build Tormore, it was their commitment to the future of the Scotch whisky industry, having taken over Long John from Sir Hugh Fraser, later Lord Fraser of Allander. This gave them a foothold in the Scotch whisky business, and they decided to expand on their acquisition by building the new malt distillery at Tormore. The celebrated architect Sir Albert Richardson was commissioned to design the buildings and the distillery village, and having seen some of his alternative plans for possible versions of Tormore, I have to say that the one that was finally chosen was not necessarily the most picturesque, though it did turn out to have a certain grandeur about it, and is now widely accepted as a classic of its kind.

The distillery itself was constructed to a very high standard, and was intended as a showpiece, but it overran its budget, so in order to make savings they cut the size of the staff houses from the original design. The manager's house, Valley Field, was cut by three feet all round, which I felt detracted from the intended overall effect.

By the time we left Islay, Kay and I had another child, Louise, who had also been adopted, and who had been with us since December 1973, when she was just two months old. By this time Jonathan was three years old. The family had been expanded, but Kim the dog had been put down after allegedly killing some hens belonging to the former Laphroaig brewer-cum-manager Tom Anderson. Tom had never really come to terms with retirement or with the Long John regime. Although he was 65, staff at Laphroaig had previously only retired if they wanted to, and Tom felt that he had been pushed out. I had never seen Kim appear even likely to kill a mouse, but on the word of Tom, she had to be put down.

Kay flew to the mainland with the two children a couple of

days before I left Islay with the furniture at the end of March. The young Port Ellen schoolmaster, Freddie Bell, who had become a friend of ours, invited me to stay with him and his wife Helen the night before I left Islay, seeing as how all our worldly goods were packed in the removal van. What I didn't know was that Freddie and Helen had bought in vast amounts of drink, and proceeded to throw the party to end all parties, even by the standards of Islay. Lots of my friends and colleagues were invited, and it was a great way to say goodbye and to thank everyone for their marvellous hospitality and friendliness during the past four years.

The party was still going on the following afternoon when I saw the MacBrayne's ferry, on which I was due to leave the island, sailing into Port Ellen. 'I think that's my ferry,' I said as it began to manoeuvre into the harbour . But this was Islay and everyone at the party was pretty relaxed about the fact. Someone eventually suggested that I phone Harold Hastie at MacBrayne's in Port Ellen and that he would take care of everything. I duly did this, only for Harold to tell me that if I wasn't at the pier in five minutes, the ferry was sailing.

I said some hurried good-byes, leapt into my car and drove like hell towards the harbour. As I came round the corner my heart sank as I saw that the boat was about 30 yards out from the quay, making headway. When Harold saw me he radioed the skipper who promptly berthed the ferry again, lowered the ramp, and allowed me to embark. I was finally leaving Islay, albeit in something of an alcoholic haze, but perhaps that was the best way.

The island had made a profound and lasting impression on me and my family, and we were genuinely sorry to be leaving, although we recognised that in my job moving on usually meant moving up, so that tempered our sorrow at going. Living on Islay was rather like attending the University of Authentic Life, and our time there had been extremely happy. Kay was quite looking forward to being back on Speyside, close to her family and friends in Elgin, but after her initial misgivings, she had grown very fond of Islay, and was genuinely sorry to be leaving what had become her little haven by the Bay of Proaig.

A force six gale was blowing as I sailed away from Islay, which was appropriate as that was the sort of weather in which I'd first seen the island, but I managed to sleep for the entire crossing to West Loch Tarbert, and woke up a mainlander once more.

Chapter 9
Speyside:
From Tormore to Luton to Glasgow

On the 1st April 1974 Kay and I moved into Valley Field, and I was now officially the manager of Tormore; the fourth in its short history. It was a place to be proud of and with the job came a £1,000 per year salary increase, which was distinctly useful with two young children to bring up.

We had been used to heavy rain at that time of year on Islay, but on Speyside it was snowing with flakes the size of 50p pieces, and just about as heavy, too. The snow drifted to 14 feet in height, completely covering cars, and there we were, newly moved in, and completely cut off from the outside world, as the A95 which passed the front of the distillery was under several feet of snow. This lasted for a week, and it even got to the stage where we received emergency air drops from RAF helicopters! It was back to the harsh reality of the north-east Scottish weather with the temperature falling to 14 degrees below freezing point. Tormore was almost 800 feet above sea level, so perhaps we shouldn't have been surprised.

Whisky was still produced during all this, however, and once the road reopened lorries came in with distillery supplies, but it was so cold that the diesel fuel froze in their tanks and the drivers had to lag the fuel line with oily rags so that the vehicles would start up again after making their deliveries. In many cases, they didn't dare switch off their engines.

When I arrived at Tormore the yields were around 2.54 gpb, which was on a par with Laphroaig at its least impressive, and considering that there were none of the problems with heavily peated malt which existed on Islay, and that this was a very modern distillery, I was rather bewildered by such poor levels of performance. Tormore had originally been equipped with two wash stills and two spirit stills, but the stillhouse capacity had been doubled at the same time as all the Laphroaig work had been done, so that there were now eight stills in total. There had originally been eight corten steel washbacks, and when expansion took place a new tun room was built with four washbacks, which had the equivalent capacity of the eight smaller ones already in place. The new tun room had been situated on the south-east side of the distillery, behind the stillhouse. Unfortunately all the storms and all the cold, wet weather hit that building, which meant that fermentation was always poor, especially in winter. Basically, it was just too cold. Anybody with any sense and any real knowledge of distilling should have known not to site a tun room there, and apparently my predecessor, Denis Nicol, had voiced his concern when it was constructed. Because the washbacks were made of steel, they didn't retain any heat from the activity of the yeast producing alcohol and carbon dioxide, whereas wooden washbacks would have held some heat, and made for more efficient fermentation. We did not, therefore, get the yield we should have expected, and to help solve the problem we introduced a little heat into the buildings by blowing warm air from fan heaters situated at ground level at one end of the building.

Tormore was also suffering from a lack of staff confidence. Everyone from the assistant manager to the yard sweeper felt some blame for being in one of the most beautiful, modern, distilleries in Scotland, yet producing the most abysmal results in terms of efficiency and cost effectiveness. This had to be addressed very quickly, as morale was at rock bottom. The first month I was there we produced yields of 2.55, which was just not good enough. We had to achieve 2.60. With fairly minor and quite simple alterations we actually hit 2.62, which thrilled me. My experience of improving yields at Laphroaig stood me in good stead, and I suspect that was why I had been sent to Tormore in the first place.

I have to say that I found it difficult to understand how morale could be so low in any workplace where there was a clerkess like Lesley Hunter, who lived in Glenlivet and was statuesque to say the least. I was five feet ten inches, and Lesley towered over me by several inches. She was easily the tallest employee at Tormore, and at least 75 percent of her appeared to be all leg. Not that I looked very often, of course. She was also an extremely nice person and very good at her job, so I just had to put up with her!

When Lesley left, we recruited Fiona Westerman, formerly Fiona Spark, prior to her marriage. Fiona was the daughter of Harvey Spark, who came from Aberlour and was a master builder. He undertook all the dirtiest and most unpopular jobs in the distilling industry on Speyside, assisted by his sons Alan and young Harvey. While DCL had its own 'flying squad' based at Parkmore, the independent distilleries relied on a body of outside contractors to work for them. As well as Harvey Spark, these included master joiners like David Godsman, a God-fearing man with a pawky sense of humour.

Old Harvey was a real character which probably helped him cope with being covered from head to toe in soot after working in a chimney, or squeezing into the flue of a still. That and the fact that he was paid quite handsomely for his work, and was also plied with a few drams to dull the unpleasant nature of some of his tasks.

Another well-known figure in the area was Ernest 'Toots'

Forsyth, who had a very good coppersmith business in Rothes, which has since been carried on by his two sons, Richard and William. It's a much larger concern now, and as well as doing coppersmithing for distilleries, they have expanded into North Sea oil fabrication work and various other ventures. 'Toots' Forsyth was like Harvey Spark, in that he had no qualms about doing dirty work, and would cheerfully go into a still that was quite hot and do a job on it. I'm sure that apart from anything else, Health & Safety legislation would prevent that sort of thing happening today. People like Harvey and Toots were part of the folklore of the whisky business at a particular time in its development, and they played their part in keeping the wheels of the industry turning.

I had first come across Harvey's daughter Fiona when she was a teenager at Aberlour High School, and on occasion used to accompany her father to Dailuaine Distillery where I was assistant manager. She had some experience of working in a distillery environment, having spent some time with William Grant's at Glenfiddich, so she was an ideal replacement for Lesley. She proved very valuable as we had just introduced in-house budgetary controls, which meant that we monitored our budget on a weekly and a monthly basis, against the budgets that had been set for the operating year by the accountancy function in Glasgow. This brought me closer to 'pure' management, rather than being an extension of the brewer and production employees at the distillery.

The brewer at Tormore was Colin Ross, who was about 25 years old; relatively young to be a brewer at a distillery of the calibre of Tormore. Colin had previously worked for Chivas Bros in Keith, and after his time at Tormore ran the Ben Nevis Distillery in Fort William, which Long John had just acquired. He also spent some time at Laphroaig and is now a director of Ben Nevis Distillery, having been appointed by the Japanese firm Nikka, who bought the distillery from Long John in 1991.

Tormore had a plant engineer, a university graduate called Fraser Allan, and this position had been introduced by Schenley to mirror their operation in the USA, where every distillery had its own engineer. There was an engineering department based in Glasgow, where there was an expanding team, put together so that we could work in-house rather than employ consultants as had been the case in the past. This proved to be very useful, as one of the problems we faced at Tormore was that we were not disposing of our effluent in a very fit and responsible manner for a modern 'flagship' distillery. Effluent which had not been treated to meet the rigorous standards of the River Purification Board could not be discharged into the River Spey, which was, of course, a mecca for fishermen.

The original effluent plant from 1959 could no longer cope with the increased capacity of the distillery, and, in fact, it was virtually obsolete. We therefore embarked on a project to build a new effluent treatment plant; a series of vast lagoons to hold the washing water, the spent lees (the residue left over after spirit distillation) and any other draff or rain water which entered the drainage system. One of the problems of effluent is that it can de-oxygenate, and aquatic life suffers as a result. What we had to do was re-oxygenate the effluent by way of aerators set up on pontoons in the primary lagoon, a system used by Schenley in the States. After several days it flowed over a weir into the secondary lagoon, where it settled for a while before the water level took it over another weir into the tertiary lagoon. From there the now re-oxygenated effluent was pumped up into final filter beds, before passing into settling tanks to allow sludge settlement prior to passing over another weir before re-entering the watercourse.

Eventually, the rich loamy sludge was pumped from the foot of the tank into a tractor-drawn tanker, and taken to be sprayed on nearby moorland. It fertilised the moor quite effectively, and a coarse grass developed. The effluent plant was known as The Shit Works, and was run by Norman Finlayson who had to put up with the unflattering nickname of The Shitter!

Despite all this, we were still having trouble meeting the stringent effluent levels demanded of us, and eventually it was agreed that we should employ a distillery chemist with a background in the food and drinks industry, someone who was conversant with current legislation regarding purified effluent disposal into watercourses. Because we were discharging into the Spey, everything we did was under the microscope and we couldn't get away with any sharp practice. In May 1975 we appointed John Adam to the post. He had worked as a chemist in an Edinburgh brewery, and also in the tallow and offal recovery field within the food industry. His task on joining the company was to produce effluent from Tormore that was to the satisfaction of the North-East of Scotland River Purification Board. Slowly but surely he managed to accomplish this task, and by the end of the year the problem was essentially solved.

What John did was to introduce small quantities of alum into the final settlement tank, which removed the last toxic products from the purified effluent. This came as a big relief, because the distillery had been under threat of closure from the local authority unless we were able to demonstrate that we were dealing with the issue effectively. With the effluent disposal problem behind us, we decided to expand John Adam's remit to include taking an interest in other areas of the production process, such as fermentation, trial distillations we had created, and also maintenance. He identified areas of our operation where improved maintenance could increase efficiency, and worked closely with Colin Ross.

In the summer of 1974, while Kay, the children and I were on holiday at Gatehouse of Fleet on the Solway Firth, I picked up a copy of *The Scotsman* and while reading it on the beach I came across the headline 'Long John comes home for £18m.' It turned out that Schenley had sold Long John to the brewing company Whitbread, for what seemed to me to be a very reasonable price. Whitbread was new to the distilling business, but by the mid-seventies it had become fashionable for brewers to diversify into whisky. Apart from Whitbread, Allied Breweries had taken over William Teacher & Sons, giving them Ardmore and Glendronach distilleries, along with the famous Teacher brand. Scottish & Newcastle Breweries owned the Isle of Jura Distillery through their whisky subsidiary Charles Mackinlay's of Leith who had also built Glenallachie on Speyside.

Whitbread had a different philosophy to Schenley regarding distilling, and the company began to replace plant engineers with people who had more of a brewing and chemical background. The engineering operation in Glasgow was scaled down as well. Fraser Allan left Tormore and went down to Glasgow where he worked on the reconstruction of the Strathclyde grain distillery. He moved on from there to take over the old firm of Archibald Macmillan, coppersmiths and engineers, and did very well with it.

Following the takeover by Whitbread, a distillery works committee was set up, with each department of the distillery represented. In a formal way this meant that the employees were being consulted and asked their opinions, and everybody got their chance to put their point of view. The establishment of this committee led to a marked improvement in morale among the staff. Instead of cutting corners to extract every drop of spirit we could, as had previously been the case, we began to work in a more orderly and measured way, and we managed to increase the yields from 2.54 into the 2.80's, which was a massive improvement. At the same time we maintained the level of total proof gallons produced. Colin Ross played a pivotal role in the process, because I delegated the practical running of the distillery to him. I involved him in more and more of the budgetary aspects of the distillery's operation too.

If the role of the distillery manager was changing quite dramatically by this time, then so was the role of the excise officer. It was no longer considered necessary to have an officer attached to each individual distillery, and the service was slowly streamlined, but there was extreme resistance to the changes on the part of the employees. There was a fear that the staff would lose their special status as a 'service within a service', that is within the Civil Service as a whole. The excisemen were only accountable to the heads of Her Majesty's Customs & Excise, not to the rest of the Civil Service, and there was a concern that they would lose the rights and privileges they had built up over the years, and become just mere civil servants. I feel that the officers of HMC&E had actually served the industry very well, although the industry didn't always think so, and that it was a retrograde step to remove the officers from distilleries in such numbers as they did. Today there is no resident officer at any distillery, and the service even phased out having one officer responsible for three or four distilleries, which was a practice they tried for a time. There is now a system of fixed penalties for distilleries which break excise rules, but I feel that the industry had more credibility when it could prove to the world that everything was being done under the auspices of Her Majesty's Officers of Customs & Excise.

●   ●   ●

As a distillery manager I was now being encouraged by our directors to think in terms of running my own business, albeit within the overall company format. This was a tremendous opportunity to gain business experience of the kind not associated with actually making whisky, and it was to stand me in good stead in the years to come. As part of this development, it was suggested that I take up a correspondence course in accountancy, and I was also sent on a two-week residential management course at Peebles Hydro Hotel in the Borders, run by the Institute of Chartered Accountants of Scotland. This course was entitled 'Management for the Young Executive', with elements on finance and accountancy, and was held in November 1974. It had attracted people from a variety of commercial backgrounds, including some from DCL, and a young Matthew Gloag, of The Famous Grouse family in Perth.

During the middle weekend of the course the Clydeside shipbuilding union activist Jimmy Reid was addressing a conference at the Peebles Hydro, and I had the good fortune to get the opportunity to sit down and chat with him. He was a fascinating man, and despite the fact that I didn't share most of his political beliefs, I did admire him and I respected his point of view. This was a time when the unions were becoming more powerful in the distilling industry, as in most industries, and one element of our course concerned dealing with unions. A lecture was therefore delivered to us by Joe Mills, General Secretary of the Transport and General Workers Union for the north-east of England. He began his speech by saying, 'Good morning gentlemen, and welcome to the world of the new poor, because that's what you are.' At that point Matthew Gloag, whose family heritage in distilling stretched back generations, shouted an indignant, 'No way!' Curiously, it was the first time I'd ever heard the expression.

Under Whitbread, the company changed in style from the American influence of Schenley back to being very British, or more accurately, very English, and no sooner had I returned to Tormore from Peebles, than I was off down south to Whitbread's massive modern 'jumbo' brewery in Luton. This was a purpose-built brewery, which also housed Whitbread's research and development department, and the company was very much at the forefront of new scientific development within the brewing industry. It was considered important that I saw what was being done there, and it was relevant to me because, of course, brewing and distilling are very similar up to the point of distillation.

The brewery was unlike anything that had existed previously, as the industry was based on traditional, family breweries, with Whitbread having started in business in 1742 in Whitecross Street in London. Whitbread expanded through acquisition, buying up Flower's and Fremlin's and many other smaller concerns. One such firm was the Edinburgh brewer Campbell, Hope & King, and the purchase caused great sadness because they closed the brewery which had produced excellent beer – my first legal pint was brewed by the company! The Luton brewery was one of three very large new plants built by Whitbread while they replaced a number of old, rural, family-owned breweries which they had acquired. Their aim was to concentrate brewing on the three sites in Luton, Wales and Lancashire.

Building jumbo breweries rather than acquiring existing smaller ones was a complete change of direction for Whitbread, and it was questionable as to whether the management of the company at that time was actually capable of running something so large; the Luton brewery had also become a fairly militant workplace. It was very automated, and was split into a number of divisions, each of which seemed to have become the power-base for what are best described as 'little dictators', who ultimately rendered the place unmanageable. Whitbread eventually took the decision to close the entire operation, which must have meant sustaining quite a financial loss. The jumbo brewery had proved a very expensive exercise. The management of the brewery did not seem in tune with the modernity of the plant and new ways of running businesses, in that, for example, the staff dining room was split into areas for different grades of employee. A grade 11 member of staff could not have lunch with a grade 13 employee. This was totally new to me, as was the fact that lunch would be accompanied by a glass or two of the company's products, and ended with the port being passed around at about three o'clock. This probably didn't contribute anything positive to industrial relations! One of the reasons for the very regimented approach to management was that most of the senior executives were ex-army officers, many of them members of the Whitbread family, and after military service they brought their army training back into the running of the company.

At the time of my visit to Luton, Whitbread had recently

begun producing lager and was brewing Heineken under licence. The move from traditional beers to lagers was well under way, and Luton was essentially just a large beer factory. My trip south was probably an attempt to imbue me with the company ethos – 'Whitwashing' as I came to think of it – much as my visit to Schenley's Cincinnati operation had been. Sadly, the scenery was not as grand, and I don't recall anyone telling me to, 'Have a nice day.'

I saw things like the training courses and the Luton experience as part of a plan for my future role within the company, and I got the impression that I was being considered as somebody with potential to go further within the organisation. Whitbread introduced formal job descriptions and an annual appraisal system, the hardest part of which was recording what you saw as your failures during the year!

One of the recurring problems we had at Tormore was with the distillery boiler, which had originally been coal-fired and had later been converted to oil. The fitter, Ronnie Fraser, was fortunately a man who would work all the hours given, night and day. He never seemed to be happy unless he was covered in grease and oil, and he always reminded me of McPhail, the engineer on the *Vital Spark* in Neil Munro's *Para Handy* stories. He had worked at another distillery before Tormore, but he also had the great advantage of being a trained motor mechanic, which came in handy for the distillery staff, whose cars he would fix for a modest consideration. He would also act as chauffeur if Kay and I were going to any formal functions, and he would drive down to Aviemore to meet the train if I had been in Glasgow on Long John or Whitbread business. He had been a piper in the army, so if he needed to let off steam you always knew about it, because he would be marching up and down the garden of his house in the distillery village, blowing fit to burst. It was Ronnie who introduced me to the theory that the best cure for a major hangover was to drink yourself sober, though I remain unconvinced.

Alec Milne – known as Ack – was one of the older staff at

Tormore, with a couple of years to go until he retired. Ack was tall, had a stoop and was balding, with three teeth strategically missing from the front of his mouth. One day he was sweeping up in the distillery when a small man with a pork pie hat on and a navy blue mackintosh down to his ankles came in. The man had a face that looked as though it had been used as a punchbag. Ack had just washed the floor, and the little man walked over it, before disappearing into the bin room. Ack was less than delighted to see footprints on his clean floor, and challenged the stranger, saying, 'Who the fuck do you think you are, you wee shite! Get out of here before I call the manager.'

The man replied in an American accent, 'And who the fuck do you think you're talking to…the Pope?'

'No,' retorted Ack, 'but I'd be better talking to the Pope. I suppose you think you're the fucking president of the USA?'

On reflection, this was probably not the friendliest way to greet Al Owen, who had come all the way from Cincinnati to see Tormore. Sensing that the little man might just be more than just a passing intruder, Ack decided to come and tell me what had happened before I found out from anyone else. He burst into my office and said, 'If you're going to give me the sack do it now. I think I've done something terrible.' When he told me what had happened I burst out laughing, and said, 'Ack, you haven't let me down, you've done what I thought you would in the circumstances. You were right to question someone you didn't know in the distillery, though the method of questioning may have been a bit unconventional.'

When Al came into my office a while later he said to me, 'Who was that goddam feller who stopped me in the bin room? Tell him from me he did a good job there, though I could have kicked his ass.' The story became a legend within Long John, and I suppose we were creating some of the early 'folklore' surrounding Tormore; as a comparatively new distillery it didn't have a lot of history.

Another Tormore character helping to make the folklore was

Willie Grant, a very rough and ready former sawmill worker, who had an extremely lived-in face, which made him look much older than his twenty-something years. He had flaming red curly hair, and a complexion to match. Willie lived in a distillery cottage, and one Saturday afternoon I was at home when I heard gunfire. Colin Ross lived in another distillery house, and he rushed out to investigate, as the sound of windows smashing could be heard. He discovered Willie Grant in his living room with a heap of logs in front of the fire, and a scene that resembled something from a Wild West film. Two window panes had been shot out, and bits of metallic debris were embedded in the living room walls. When I subsequently interviewed Willie about all of this he told me that he had bought the load of logs from the sawmill at Dulnain Bridge where he had once worked, and that forestry workers sometimes put small charges into big trees in order to split them, to save work with saws and axes. Some of these, he suggested, must have been left in the batch of logs he had purchased. This seemed a tall story, particularly considering the length of time the 'gunfire' seemed to have lasted, but I had no choice but to accept his version of events. He was handed a bill for several hundred pounds for repairs to the cottage, and eventually he was able to agree with me with a rueful chuckle that it had been an expensive load of logs. Poaching wasn't exactly unknown in the area, and my theory about the incident is that Willie had hidden a stash of shotgun cartridges in the fireplace and had completely forgotten about them.

In 1975 it was decided to upgrade the interior of the distillery, which by this time badly needed it. Funds had not been forthcoming from Schenley to do this because they probably had it in their heads that Tormore was a 'new' distillery. We fitted a new production floor and removed the glass walls which separated the original tun room from the stillhouse and mash house. We had to dismantle the large panes of glass in the dividing walls while production continued, and then put in guardrails, as the tun room had a higher floor level than the areas on either side of it. We also fitted an umbrella-like stainless-steel canopy a couple of feet above the mash tun which allowed us to observe the mash as in the old days when fully open mash tuns were the norm. Efficient vapour extraction systems meant we were not subjected to Turkish bath conditions!

We installed a temperature-controlled cold store in which to keep our yeast, and one of the practical developments that had come out of my visit to Luton was the idea that rather than just discarding the yeast used in brewing, it could perhaps be recycled into the company's distilleries. Bill Brown was now production director of Long John International, and he and I visited Whitbread's Castle Eden brewery in County Durham, in order to examine the logistics of the yeast recycling proposition. It was envisaged that, if practical, the yeast would be used not only at Tormore, but also at Long John's Glenugie Distillery at Peterhead, and perhaps even at Laphroaig. I can't say that we were very impressed by the type of yeast we were going to receive, which looked too wet and hadn't been pressed nearly enough, and I doubted whether it would travel well.

We duly took delivery of our first consignment of the yeast, which was literally running out of the bags when we got it off the lorry; there was no point in putting it into our new cold store because it had 'blown'. It was virtually useless, but we used it anyway, because we had to see what results we got, and, predictably, the results were not good. What we did was use it in a mixture with pure culture yeast, produced in a factory by the DCL. We tried it two or three times, but it was never a success, although obviously it had seemed a worthwhile idea, and would have made economic sense if it had meant that Long John didn't have to buy in brewers' yeast from outside sources.

A few days after my trip to Castle Eden Brewery, a Whitbread van dropped off a crate of small bottles of beer at Tormore, accompanied by a 'with compliments' slip from Brian Spencer, who was the brewer at Castle Eden. It was a Friday afternoon, and nothing much was happening at the distillery, so I went home around 4.30 with my crate of beer, determined to slake my thirst at the end of a very hot June day. I went into the playroom where the children were watching television, sat down and opened one of the little bottles of beer. It went down pretty well, so I had a second, after which I called Kay through from the kitchen and told her that I thought there was something wrong with the television, as the picture was blurring and some of the images were doubling. She suggested that the strong sunlight might have affected my eyes, and returned to the kitchen. I duly drank a third beer, and then shouted for Kay again, as there was now most certainly something wrong with the television. In fact with the televisions, as there were two of them, side by side. We also appeared to have four children.

'What on earth is in that beer you're drinking?', Kay asked suspiciously. She picked up one of the empty bottles and looked at the label. 'No wonder you're seeing two of everything,' she said, 'this stuff's is eight percent alcohol.' That was more than twice the strength of an average beer, and explained a lot. This was my first introduction to Whitbread's barley wine. I took the precaution of switching off the television before finishing the crate.

Because it was reckoned to be such a showpiece distillery, Tormore attracted visiting groups from all over the world. On one occasion we were entertaining a Finnish party, and after a buffet lunch in the recreation hall, I was making a short speech to them as I usually did, when I got my suns mixed up, and welcomed, 'Our visitors from the Land of the Rising Sun.' There was a deathly silence, which puzzled me. It was only after the group had left the distillery that I realised what I had said, and that Finland was the 'Land of the Midnight Sun'.

Rainbow trout had been introduced to the distillery dam, partly to make it look attractive to visitors, but also because they helped to purify the water that was going to go down into the distillery as process water. As the first point of any tour, we would take visitors up to the dam to show them our water supply, and they could see how clear the water was. While I was at Tormore we improved access to the dam, clearing out some old trees on the banks, planting them with alpine shrubs, and widening the gravel paths. We laid crazy paving around the dam itself from stones hacked out of the banking and created a kind of Japanese garden. This was a fairly major landscaping project, but it improved the initial perception visitors got of the distillery and its environs. We were praised by people from all over the world for the work we had done, and it helped to complement the showpiece aspect of the actual distillery buildings.

In addition to Tormore distillery itself, we owned what was effectively a small estate of 600 acres, and that had to be managed too, which took up quite a bit of my time. We were socially accountable for not only our production processes and the distillery complex, but also for the land around it, and we were responsible for the wellbeing of a community, which numbered around 20 people. We had an informal arrangement with the gamekeepers of surrounding estates, and particularly the Seafield Estate, which was the largest in the area, that if anyone was shooting on their land and the game came across onto our ground, they could follow it. I always knew when this had happened, as I would arrive home from work to discover a present such as a brace of pheasants, a salmon, or a haunch of venison waiting for me.

It looked as though our family would be staying at Tormore for the foreseeable future, and we settled down well, paying a Saturday afternoon visit to Elgin each week to shop and see Kay's parents. Meanwhile Jonathan had started school in Grantown. We were encouraged by the company to consider buying a house in the area, perhaps in Grantown or Aberlour, in order to get into the property market, and although we were relatively well off in terms of our total remuneration package, which included a free company house, as the taxman began to take more and more interest in benefits in kind, that became less attractive. We were to find when we began to look at the cost of buying a house of our own that we had been cushioned from some of the realities that faced most families of our age.

Tormore was in many ways an ideal place in which to bring up a young family, for there were private roads around the distillery, which were useful as the children were now learning to ride bicycles. There were, however, also dangers. A hundred yards from the house was a pond the size of a double curling rink and about three feet deep. One day I was summoned from my office by a barrage of screams and lots of splashing. Jonathan had gone head over heels off his bike into the pond, and one of the distillery workers was in the process of rescuing him! He emerged unharmed, but didn't need warning about the pond again and kept well away from it in future.

A minor, but perpetual, irritation for us at Tormore was the flagpole, which stood close to our house and on which we used to hoist the appropriate national flag of any visiting party from overseas. The rope would bang against the pole even in quite light winds, and keep you awake at night. This was nothing, however, compared to the clock. When Richardson had designed Tormore along lavish lines, he incorporated a beautiful clock which played Scottish tunes. The drawback was that it played them every quarter of an hour. Even the most ardent patriot would have tired of hearing *Highland Laddie* at 3.30 in the morning, and again at 3.45. And again at four o'clock, ad infinitum. Eventually we got the clockmaker who had installed it to come up from Derby and adapt it so that it only played a tune every hour, and was silent during the night. The happy day also came when the flagpole had rotted sufficiently to justify replacement with a fibreglass version and a polished steel cable instead of a hemp rope. For a while it was impossible to sleep because of the silence.

If Tormore seemed a good place to bring up children, it also seemed a good place to have another dog, and in the summer of 1976 we acquired a puppy from a litter of Dalmatians bred by the local area surveyor of customs and excise, Teddy Francis. We got a liver-spotted pup called Cassius, or Cass for short, and he rapidly became a great favourite with the children. He needed an enormous amount of exercise, so we stopped spending Saturday afternoons shopping, and they became occasions for long walks on the moor with Cass and the children. We were very lucky to be bringing up our children in a situation so far removed from all that was bad in society, and my Saturday afternoons with them and an apparently tireless dog became very special for me.

● ● ●

In the summer of 1976 a problem developed in our sister distillery of Glenugie, at Peterhead, which at that time was the most easterly distillery in Scotland. Glenugie's manager, Sandy Auchinachie, was absent from duty due to ill-health, and the distillery was being looked after by the brewer, Ken Philips, who had once worked at Tormore. The problem was a fairly major oil spill which had occurred with the heavy crude oil which was supplied to the distillery for use in the burners of the boilers to raise steam. There was an automatic alarm system which was designed to warn when the level of the oil rose too high in the tank. It had failed and the oil had ended up on the beach; the battle lines were drawn between the whisky industry and the conservation lobby.

I was sent up to Peterhead to have a look at the situation, and it was not a pretty sight. The beach was quite extensively contaminated, along with the distillery watercourse which flowed into the sea. Our first priority was to ensure that production was not stopped, because the company needed the spirit, and it was my view that Colin Ross should go to Glenugie and take day-to-day control of the distillery. Ken Philips had got into quite a state over the whole matter, believing that it was his responsibility, even though he was adamant that the automatic alarm had not worked. Apart from anything else, I felt it would be very good experience for Colin. This duly happened, and Colin and I subsequently had a meeting with representatives of the RPB and conservationists. I had discussed with Bill Brown, our production director in Glasgow, what approach we should take, and it was decided to get a professional cleaning company in to sort things out, with Long John picking up the tab.

Some years later, Glenugie was closed down by Long John International, partly because it was felt that its capacity was surplus to requirements in the early eighties, when there was a general world-wide depression which hit the whisky industry hard. Another reason for its closure was that the company had just bought back the original home of Long John, Ben Nevis Distillery at Fort William, and they proceeded to strip some of the plant out of Glenugie and relocate it to Ben Nevis. At the time, the North Sea oil boom, based around Aberdeen and Peterhead, was at its height, and with commercial property at a premium, Glenugie Distillery became the base for North Sea oil engineering companies. This seems rather ironic, considering our problems there with the black stuff a few years earlier.

The absence of Colin Ross at Glenugie for some weeks enabled me to work more closely at Tormore with the chemist John Adam, and to try to point him in the direction of a more managerial role within the company. Out of a negative situation, we got two positives, in that Colin gained valuable experience away from Tormore, and John's time working closely with me helped him to look towards new horizons. I also got to go back to a more 'hands-on' style of management for a while, and this was made easier by the fact that we now had Bill Rattray as our administration assistant. Bill had owned and ran a traditional licensed grocery and off-licence business in Grantown, and having sold up he came to Tormore to replace Fiona, who wanted to move on to pastures new. Fiona had done a wonderful job, but Bill was able to expand the role, and offer me even more administrative support.

When I first entered the whisky business the average distillery summer 'silent season' lasted for about three months, during which repairs and maintenance work were done. By 1976, such was the demand on distilleries to produce spirit in quantity, that our silent season at Tormore only lasted for a fortnight. It was reckoned that around the same time Glenfiddich Distillery had a silent season of just three days, which would hardly have been long enough to cool the stills!

One piece of work which was scheduled to be done during the silent season was the de-scaling of the tubes in the water boiler and a Glasgow company had been brought in by John Adam to do the job. John was having problems getting the work done to the agreed timescale, and one evening he asked the workman to finish the job so that the boiler could be fired up next morning and production resume. The man replied, 'Listen you, I've got a bath of acid in front of me, and if you don't shut up and get off my back all they'll find of you in the morning will be your teeth.' Perhaps we just weren't used to that quaint Glaswegian humour up on Speyside, but it sounded like a pretty serious threat to John, who was alone with this man after dark in the distillery. I made an official written complaint to the managing director of the company doing the work, and he responded by stating that his man had felt a bit under pressure and his remark had only been intended as a joke. We remained unconvinced, and if anyone mentioned acid or Glaswegians in John Adam's company during the next few weeks he visibly blanched, even though he came from Glasgow himself.

During that short silent season we were also replacing sections of some of the stills, and because of the design of the stillhouse, the only way you could get pieces of still in and out was to remove the very large window in the gable end of the main building. We duly did this, and replaced the head, swan neck and lyne arm of one of the wash stills. We had brought in the firm of coppersmiths called Abercrombie from Alloa to do the job. Abercrombie was a subsidiary of DCL, having been acquired by them many years previously to produce and repair the company's stills 'in house'. I had worked with Abercrombie in my DCL days, so I knew some of the company's personalities quite well. We were due to start the distillery up again with everything finished by a certain deadline, and we had begun mashing a few days in advance of the deadline, so it was essential we got the stills fired up on time. The head of the still fitted perfectly onto the body, and the swan neck fitted the head, but unfortunately the flange on the swan neck didn't quite match up with the flange on the lyne arm – it was slightly off centre and wouldn't bolt together. The people from Abercrombie's said they would have to take the whole thing apart and start again, but because of our timescale this simply wasn't an option. I told Joe McLaughlin, the coppersmith on site, that he would have to get it working in situ, and he duly came into my office and phoned his boss back in Alloa. His boss obviously suggested that he perform some sort of balancing act up on the lyne arm in order to make adjustments, because Joe became progressively more agitated as the conversation went on. Finally he lost it totally, and shouted down the phone, 'Christ George, what do you want me to do, stick feathers in my arse and flee, you daft bugger!' I was convulsed with laughter which helped to relieve some of the tension...for me, at any rate. Joe looked at me incredulously, and said, 'I'm glad you think it's so bloody funny', before marching back into the stillhouse to carry out his boss's instructions. We rapidly constructed a small scaffolding up the back of the still head as far as the underside of the offending flange, and Joe then worked his coppersmithing magic until late into the night. Feathers were not required after all. We were able to start distilling again next day, but it had been a close run thing.

●　　　●　　　●

While I was at Tormore we conducted an interesting experiment in terms of cask storage: the first palletised storage project in the Scotch whisky industry. We converted one of the original warehouses with earth floor and wooden runners, by laying down a reinforced concrete floor. We worked out how many pallets the warehouse could hold, each containing nine barrels standing on end, taking into account stresses and pressure points. We were able to stack five pallets high in the middle of the warehouse where the roof reached its highest point over the ground, with three pallets closest to the walls where the roof was at its lowest. This meant a doubling of the capacity of the warehouse. We could, of course, only move casks in and out with a fork-lift truck, and we had one specially made, which ran on propane gas, scrubbed through a filter, so that there were no fumes in the warehouse to disturb the delicate micro-climate in which the spirit was maturing. This project was the forerunner of Long John International's construction of very large warehouses within its Westthorn complex in Glasgow some years later. It has now been copied by several other distillers, and is simply a more efficient use of space. One practical drawback, however, was that selecting sequentially numbered casks was a practical nightmare. It was almost impossible to draw casks in the order which the blender, for example, often wanted.

At Tormore we disposed of our pot ale or spent wash by road tanker to a processing plant near Glenfarclas Distillery, about ten miles further along the A95. The remains of that plant, now derelict, can still be seen, although trees obscure most of it from the road. The company which ran the plant traded as BFP – Ballindalloch Feed Products –a consortium formed by Long John, J&G Grant of Glenfarclas, and the Aberlour Distillery. Aberlour belonged at that time to House of Campbell, which was virtually owned outright by Arnold Campbell and his family and subsequently taken over by Pernod-Ricard. The wet draff was also taken into the Balindalloch plant to produce distillers' dark grains, which had become more popular as an animal feedstuff in its own right, as well as a feedstuff supplement. This was one way of disposing of the most toxic of our effluent, and it had the added advantage of turning it into something that could be sold on. Unfortunately for BFP, the process was difficult and costly, which meant that is was hard for them to make a profit. Before my time at Tormore, the manager of BFP had been a man by the name of Charlie Candy, which was quite apt, since the spent wash looked like candy when it was being dried, and the whole place had the smell of a toffee works about it. The consortium that ran BFP decided to appoint a manager with more technical qualifications in an attempt to make the operation profitable, and the job went to Bill MacFadzean, a chemical engineer from ICI. I identified with one of the problems faced by BFP, as it related to the discharge of the final effluent into the nearby burn, which in turn flowed into the River Spey. Bill worked tirelessly under very trying conditions, as he had to satisfy three masters, all with different attitudes to capital and revenue expenditure, and sometimes negative attitudes to any expenditure at all. The weight of his technical arguments did, however, convince any doubters that money must be spent on the plant in order to bring about profitability. Sadly, Bill died suddenly while still in his forties, and didn't live to see the positive end-result of all his efforts.

From time to time the managers of the three distilleries involved in BFP were invited to lunch in the recently opened visitor reception centre at Glenfarclas, following board meetings. Grant's of Glenfiddich had, of course, operated a successful visitor centre for some years, and the 'tourist route' was one being taken by a number of distilleries around that time. This was the beginning of what was later to become the 'Whisky Trail', which now takes in a number of leading distilleries and the Speyside Cooperage at Craigellachie. During our lunches at Glenfarclas there was always a sense that most people felt distilling had more or less been invented on Speyside, and was peculiar to that part of the world. While it had undoubtedly become the foremost distilling centre in Scotland, Speyside was far from being the birthplace of Scotch whisky, with distilling probably coming to Scotland from Ireland by way of the Kintyre peninsula.

By early 1977, Kay and I were about to plunge into the housing market, having found a property we liked in Grantown-on-Spey, when I received a phone call from Bill Brown in Glasgow, inviting Kay and I to the annual dinner dance of BFP in the Craig Lyne Hotel in Grantown. An hour before the start of the event he asked Kay and I to go up to his hotel room, offered us a dram, and announced that Long John in Glasgow had been looking at what he called 'the succession plans' for the company, and that I should put on hold any intention I had of buying a house. I had been identified as a player in the succession plan, which would mean a move to Glasgow, and Bill Brown told us that the job he had in mind for me was Quality Assurance Manager of Long John. This would be a functional management rather than a line-management job, and there was a philosophy within Whitbread that if you reached a certain level of management in any of the operating companies, then you were interchangeable at that level, regardless of whether the company was producing spirits or beer, whether it was a distribution company, or even something like the newly-created Beefeater Steak House division.

In my new role I would be based at the warehousing, blending and bottling plant of Westthorn. Many years previously, it had been Bill Brown who had identified what was then Westthorn Farm on London Road in Glasgow as a potential site for the Long John operation. When he joined the company it had consisted of just Glenugie and the old Strathclyde distilleries, but by now Strathclyde had been redeveloped, incorporating a small malt whisky-producing plant called Kinclaith, Laphroaig had been acquired, Tormore had been constructed, and the Westthorn complex had been created. Bill Brown had been very instrumental in all of this, in building the history of Long John, from its days of Long John Distillers, through the Schenley period, and now into the ownership of Whitbread as Long John International.

There were two large free-standing signboards at the entrance to Tormore, one of which displayed the MacDonald coat of arms used by the company, as 'Long John' MacDonald – so called because of his height – had been the founder of the original Ben Nevis Distillery in Fort William. It was historically very apt that the company should later re-purchase Ben Nevis and run it again for a while. Being so conscious of the background of the company, Bill Brown decided it would be a nice touch to use one of the signboards at Tormore to give some of the history of the distillery, stating when it was opened and by whom, and listing all the managers. He duly did this, but sadly, after he retired in late 1977, the Whitbread hierarchy removed both the boards, as they presumably decided they wanted no reference to what had gone on before they took charge. I always thought that was rather petty, especially for a company the size of Whitbread, and one which was so keen to stress its family and traditional values. It seemed rather mean and short-sighted to try to deny Tormore its history in that way.

I had very mixed feelings about the prospect of moving to Glasgow, and I asked Bill Brown whether it was really necessary to go, as we were very happy at Tormore, but he said that staying there would do my career prospects no good, and that he felt there was a great future for me in the company. When I suggested that perhaps I was content to be where I was, and maybe didn't want to 'progress' in the company, it was made abundantly clear by Bill that if I didn't go to Glasgow I wouldn't be going anywhere, and I certainly wouldn't be staying at Tormore, come what may! I was flattered to be offered the promotion, of course, and to be thought of as someone who could go places in the organisation, but I had no great wish to live in Glasgow, and neither did Kay. As far as the children were concerned, there would be no more opportunities for Louise to feed young deer from her hand as she was able to do at Tormore, and Jonathan wouldn't be able to go riding regularly, as he did at a farm near Rothes every

Sunday morning, where his pony was appropriately called Whisky. Kay and I were concerned that the whole 'natural' aspect of their upbringing would be lost in the city, but there wasn't much we could do about the situation.

I was invited down to Glasgow to meet the directors of the company, and in particular Douglas Heard, who was responsible for commercial activities and quality control within Long John. He gave me an idea of what would be required of me in the new post they were creating, which was to encompass quality control as part of the quality assurance function. Quality assurance meant ensuring that the entire operation, from cereal selection to packaging and distribution of the end product, performed to the highest level. Quality control was the instrument used to measure most aspects of production.

It was envisaged that I would move to Glasgow in the summer of 1977, so I had to begin looking for a property to purchase. I found that house prices in the city were disturbingly high compared to Grantown. A spacious four-bedroomed house with a nice garden in Grantown had been going to cost us £12,000, while the same sort of house in a reasonable area of Glasgow was going for three times that price. We had to scale down our aspirations somewhat, and eventually bought half of a converted villa with two to three bedrooms in Pollockshields. It cost us £16,700, and wasn't a patch on the Grantown house, but it was all we could afford. It put a whole new perspective on Glasgow being the 'dear green place'. It was also expected by certain members of the company that your children would go to a fee-paying school, which meant that the salary increase was going to have to be substantial if we were to afford it all. Inevitably, it wasn't very impressive, and I was quite disappointed. I felt that the whole thing had not been well thought out by the company, who had, after all, told me that I could expect to be at Tormore for much more than just three years.

It came as a great culture shock to the system to be living in

Glasgow after the relative tranquillity of Tormore, and I also became aware of company politics for the first time, when a senior manager of the company phoned me and told me he didn't know why I had been appointed, as there was already a perfectly competent quality control manager in Glasgow! Clearly the knives were out early. I had been shielded from all of this by being based at a distillery, and in Glasgow I met a different sort of animal who stalked the corridors of company headquarters. It soon became clear that diplomacy with my colleagues was going to be as vital as actually doing my job. I had no interest in the politics of the situation, but I became aware that I would have to learn some new skills if I was to survive in this quite alien world, though I felt very disillusioned at the necessity.

My replacement at Tormore was John Adam, which disappointed Colin Ross, who had been there much longer than John, but I knew that Colin's day was coming, and that it would not be too long before he received his reward for all the hard work he had done. My loyalties were somewhat divided, because although I had no doubt John could do the job, and that his experience before joining the company would stand him in good stead, I had helped Colin to develop his skills and his self-confidence during the time we worked together.

Before we left Tormore, the staff threw a surprise party for us. As it was July, it took the form of an open-air event, staged on the patio area which we had landscaped around the dam. They had decked it out with fairy lights, and there was plenty of singing and dancing to accompany the consumption of copious amounts of whisky. The venue might have proved an unwise one, but luckily no one drank so much that they fell into the dam, and it didn't even rain that evening. We were presented with a beautiful standard lamp – the result of a staff collection. This was the first time such a thing had happened to me, and I was very touched by it.

Chapter 10
Glasgow:
Scotch & Plymouth Gin

I had experienced city life in Edinburgh as a young man, but after so long living in comparatively remote places, moving to Glasgow felt like forsaking paradise for hell. We all found it difficult to adjust, and Jonathan hated his new school, running away on a number of occasions. Cass, the Dalmatian, clearly thought this was a fairly sound plan, and proceeded to follow suit. Eventually Cass was traced to the animal shelter in Cardonald, and we were able to reclaim him, but a cramped first-floor flat was hardly the ideal place for an energetic young dog, nor, for that matter, for an energetic young family. Cass ran away again, and eventually we found a new home for him with a delightful lady in Wishaw, who loved Dalmatians and had a large walled garden. I asked her if she would take the rest of us too, but she declined.

My new role as quality assurance manager was difficult to get to grips with; in the past I had been in charge of my own operation as a line manager, but now found I could not issue direct instructions to line managers and their staff. I felt in something of a vacuum, because there I was in Glasgow, responsible for quality assurance in distilleries which were mostly a considerable distance away. Strathclyde Distillery was on our doorstep, but it was 160 miles to Laphroaig by air and 200 miles to Tormore by road, while Glenugie was a similar distance away. I was also responsible for the company's Plymouth Gin brand. I didn't even bother to work out how far away Plymouth was! Having been on the other side of the fence, as distillery manager, I knew how remote the Glasgow end of the operation seemed, and I knew it would not be easy to get my views and ideas across to the men running the individual plants. Until very recently, I had been working on the same footing as these people, and now I had to put over the company's official line on quality to them.

At first I worked alongside Douglas Heard, who was about to retire from his role as quality controller, but stayed on for a while to show me the ropes. Any ideas I came up with had to be referred to Douglas for approval, and all I could really do was to offer recommendations. The aim was to suggest changes to procedures which might improve aspects of quality. This would also hopefully be reflected in greater cost-effectiveness. I missed having my own show, as it were, to run. For the first time in ten years I wasn't in charge of an operation which was making something. I had to share an office, and I couldn't just get up and go and talk to my staff as they went about their tasks, or even walk through the distillery and look at how the mashes were coming on.

It was a painful period of adjustment, and while I was determined to make a success of my new role, I was very aware that there were people within the company in Glasgow who didn't think it was right that someone from the 'sticks' should have been brought in over the heads of existing Glasgow staff. Over the years, little empires within empires had been created, and I wanted to sweep them away. My aim was to create an atmosphere where everybody felt they had a part to play, and could say what they wanted in a meeting without fear or favour. I was influenced in this by the works committee which had been established at Tormore, and I set up a system of morning meetings where I got together informally with people like the blender, the chief scientist, the head chemist and the project chemist, so that they could all have their say.

I shared my office with a man in his early fifties called John Sloan. John was a production engineer and cost accountant, who had worked for Rolls-Royce in East Kilbride and had run his own engineering company for a while, before it succumbed to the slump of the early seventies. He had also worked in the States for a time. Although he seemed to be a bit of a West of Scotland rough diamond, this was deceptive, because he had been to the Harvard Business School! Long John had hired him to carry out project work regarding the efficiency of the bottling complex, the blending plant and the warehousing operation. Not surprisingly, he was viewed with a degree of hostility by the various managers of these areas of activity. They felt affronted that it was even considered necessary to employ someone to do this job. John and I speculated that we had been asked to share an office because we were both looked upon with great suspicion by just about everybody else on the site.

John was a rabid Rangers football fan, and I soon became acutely aware of the divisions in Glasgow symbolised by allegiances to football clubs. To an outsider, it looked pretty much like tribal warfare. I found it bizarre that here we all were working for a company, in which loyalties were split roughly three to two in favour of Celtic as opposed to Rangers, and the fervour of the support was astonishing. For someone who had spent so much of his time on Speyside, I could only conclude that Rothes never enjoyed such devotion in the Highland League.

The level of absenteeism in many places of work in Glasgow was directly related to the performances of Celtic and Rangers, and the Westthorn site was no exception. It was bad enough if one of the Glasgow teams was beaten by, say, Aberdeen, on the Saturday, when a considerable number of workers would not be well enough to turn up on Monday. By far the worst situation, however, came when there was an Old Firm Celtic-Rangers derby match. Then it didn't matter who won, there would be a lot of empty places at work when the new week began. Productivity could be appalling after an Old Firm game, and it was very difficult to try to explain this phenomenon to anyone who didn't know Glasgow. Unfortunately, that included most of the senior staff of Whitbread.

One of the reasons for increasing automation in the plant was to combat the effects of staff absences, and it became imperative that the company got the unions positively involved in helping to reduce absenteeism. With co-operation from the half dozen unions represented on the site, the company eventually 'bought out' the staff sick pay scheme, which was seen by many workers as a means of obtaining an extra fortnight's paid holiday each year. A cash incentive was offered in exchange, and subsequently anybody with a poor attendance record due to sickness could be referred to the company doctor for assessment.

By 1977 the new Strathclyde Distillery was complete, and its project manager, Mike Walker was appointed distillery manager. Perhaps the most relaxing time Mike had spent during the five years of construction was when he accompanied me to the USA and Canada. I had noticed his hair turn from light grey to snow white during those five years! Even when the distillery reopened, Mike could not sit back and breathe a sigh of relief as there were initial problems with the new distillation plant. The plant was quite revolutionary, in that its fermenting vessels were located outside the distillery buildings. They were made from stainless steel, and in hot weather they got too hot too quickly. We arranged a system of spraying cooling water around the top of them so that the process of fermentation could take place at its optimum temperature. Conversely, in winter we struggled to keep them warm enough. Even today, most distilleries have their fermenters contained within the building, and it isn't too difficult to see why. The entire plant had been designed by Schenley, who were used to having fermenters in the open air in the USA, but it wasn't such a good idea in Glasgow.

We received quite a number of complaints about Strathclyde Distillery from local residents in the Gorbals, who objected to the steam, smell and noise, particularly at night. On one occasion a public meeting was organised at which representatives of the company were to meet aggrieved residents, and I was invited to take part. Duncan McGregor, our production director, then announced that he had a pressing engagement elsewhere, and when I discovered that Mike Walker would also not be present, I realised that I had been set up. The mood of the meeting was initially quite aggressive, until the residents' spokeswoman, a Mrs Harrity, got up and said indignantly, 'I'd just like fer tae say that if Mr McDougall would spend a night wi' me, he'd find oot whit it was like.' Politely, I declined, amid general laughter, after which the atmosphere of the meeting improved markedly. We subsequently held another meeting, attended by Frank McElhone, who was MP for the Glasgow Gorbals. Residents' concerns were further addressed and it took place in a Portakabin on the distillery site. Half-way through the meeting some of the local kids started pelting the hut with bricks and lumps of cement. This was in no way a political gesture, it was just the sort of thing that happened of an evening in that part of the city.

Long John did everything it was legally obliged to in order to reduce inconvenience for people who lived in the area and the Residents' Association was pleased that the company was prepared to meet them and discuss problems. There was, however, a large block of flats situated close by the distillery chimney and those living in the topmost flats inevitably got the shortest straw.

When I arrived in Glasgow, new stainless-steel column stills (replacing the old-fashioned Coffey stills) were just being commissioned at Strathclyde, and a large part of the increased production of Strathclyde spirit was used as 'barter currency' with other distillers. Capacity had been increased from around 15 million lpa per annum to 30 million lpa, and the financial investment had been very high. It was imperative, therefore, that the quality of spirit produced was sufficiently good not just to please Long John, but to impress the trade at large. This allowed reciprocal trading to occur, and meant that we could acquire additional malt whiskies for the Long John blends.

The Coffey stills had contained a series of copper, perforated plates, over which the alcoholic liquid passed during fractionation, but the new stainless steel columns contained no copper. It proved very difficult trying to match the quality standard of the old Strathclyde spirit with that of the new, both for our own use and that of our customers, who included Bell's and Lawson's. No matter how the new stills were set, they produced 'rubbery' or 'sulphury' spirit.

One day I had to go along to Bell's plant at Broxburn, where there was a line of tankers in the yard filled with the produce of Strathclyde, which Bell's blending manager had rejected. All we could do was return the spirit to Glasgow and submit it for re-distillation. Inevitably, my role as quality assurance manager placed quite a strain on my good working relationship with Mike Walker. Whitbread had appointed a chief scientist called Mike Jackson to work within Long John, so I found myself playing 'piggy in the middle' between them, quite often over the issue of Strathclyde spirit quality. By this time, Whitbread was taking a great practical interest in Long John, flexing its muscles not only in the distilleries, but also in the areas of maturation, blending, bottling, packaging and transportation. At this time the company made a number of appointments at a very senior level, and it was clear that Whitbread wanted to stamp both its authority and character on the Long John operation.

We conducted exhaustive laboratory tests at Strathclyde, and it was felt that perhaps the lack of copper in the system was to blame for the poor results. The problem was eventually cured by inserting pure copper chains into the feints tanks. It seemed a very simple solution in a hi-tech world, but it worked. It proved once again that sometimes old methods should be respected and not allowed to become redundant. The copper hadn't been in the old Coffey stills merely for decoration; the chemical reaction between copper and distillate contributed to the acceptability of the spirit. Schenley used stainless steel in the USA, and while it might have been fine for bourbon, it certainly wasn't for Scotch. Finding a solution to the problem took a great deal off our shoulders, and Mike Walker and I had a few happy drams together to celebrate.

●　　●　　●

Despite the distance between Glasgow and Plymouth, I came to thoroughly enjoy my involvement with the company's Plymouth gin operation. Plymouth Gin cannot be produced anywhere other than in Plymouth, as it is a generic product rather than a style, unlike London gin, which can be made anywhere. It was refreshing to be able to go down to Plymouth and be back 'on site' in a distillery, albeit not a 'proper' distillery, as serious whisky men would see it. It was also a trip back to my roots in one sense, as my great grandfather came from the Devon village of Lifton. The manager at Long John's Plymouth plant was a lovely bloke called Bert Roberts, a Devonian who knew anybody and everybody in the area. As well as gin, the plant could produce vodka, and on one occasion the very prestigious London wine merchant Grants of St James sent their buyer, Angela Muir, down to Plymouth to consider our suitability to produce their own-label Romanoff vodka. I was asked to appear at the distillery a couple of days before the visit was due to take place, just to make sure everything was as it should be. I was left in no doubt that this would be an extremely good contract to win.

I duly flew down to Plymouth, and before long everything was sorted to our satisfaction. Luncheon was to take place in the Mayflower Restaurant, which overlooks Drake's Island in Plymouth Sound. Duncan McGregor planned to fly down via Gatwick in order to preside over the visit. Unfortunately, he missed his connection, but made a snap decision to charter a private executive aircraft in order to get to the meeting, which showed the importance he placed on the occasion. Duncan arrived at the distillery just as we were leaving for lunch after having taken Angela Muir on a tour of the plant. Our meeting had gone well, and she seemed satisfied that we could produce the quantity of vodka required to the standard required, and it was really a case of discussing details over lunch. Duncan prided himself on choosing the correct wines to accompany any meal, but as Angela Muir was a MW, he was tactful enough to ask her if she would make the choices. She duly did, and we all settled down to a civilised meal, with the help of a couple of excellent bottles.

Duncan and Angela were sitting opposite to Bert Roberts and myself, and just as we were starting on the fish course, Duncan kicked me very hard on my shin underneath the table, and gestured with his eyes to Bert who was knocking back a rather delicate white wine as if he was downing a pint of ale, then helping himself to a refill, then another and then another. He quaffed so much, so quickly that we had to order up another bottle pronto. This behaviour, of course, could have been interpreted either as a flattering endorsement of Angela's choice or as a severe social embarrassment. The pain I was experiencing in my lower leg clearly showed that Duncan's view was the latter. (Bert usually punctuated his morning's work with a large glass or two of Plymouth Gin, and perhaps had come to the lunch without sufficient refreshment.) I transferred the pain from my leg to Bert's ribs, via a discreetly placed elbow, and this, along with Duncan's suggestion that Bert should take charge of making sure the wine circulated around the table, got us out of a tricky situation. Angela was too much of a lady to let us see whether or not she was aware of what was happening; if she had noticed, it can't have done us much harm, because we did get the contract from Grant's to produce their vodka.

I decided to accompany Duncan in the executive plane back to Gatwick despite discovering that the runway at Plymouth was a grass strip! Duncan had been a Fleet Air Arm pilot, and so the whole exercise delighted him, filling him with nostalgia. Before we left, the pilot pointed out a cabinet with a wide selection of drinks for our use. 'We've even got a bottle of your own whisky', he announced proudly. 'It is Teacher's isn't it?' We smiled gratefully, and Duncan puffed on one of the large cigars he used to smoke in those days. 'I think, John,' he said gravely, 'we're just going to have to be a wee bit brave here,' as he unscrewed the cap and poured us both a couple of gentleman's drams.

On another occasion, I was in Plymouth on gin business when the distillery was hosting an evening reception for the Devonport Services Field Gunnery Crew, which had just emerged triumphant from that year's series of gun-pulling contests staged at the Royal Tournament in London. Plymouth Gin was a sponsor of the gun crew, hence the reception. The distillery was in the heart of the oldest part of Plymouth, and the function took place in the distillery's magnificent refectory room. This was a much older building than most of those surrounding it and was where the Pilgrim Fathers reputedly had had their last meal before setting off for the New World. Some years later, Whitbread decided in their infinite wisdom that it would be a good idea to convert this historic location into a Beefeater Steakhouse, complete with a glass wall so that diners could overlook the still room of the gin distillery.

The MD of Long John International was Ian Coombs, who was based in London and he duly made the journey down to Plymouth that evening in order to make a presentation to the gun crew. In making his speech of welcome he informed the crew members that they should avail themselves of the free bar provided by the company. The men had been in strict training for several months, and hadn't touched a drink for a long time. Despite the obvious temptation, this was the heart of naval England and nobody wanted to be the first to get up and go to the bar. Eventually one of the wives took the plunge, which signalled the start of some very serious drinking. It developed into one of the best parties I have ever been to. Well, one of the best south of the Border, at any rate! The evening ended with Ian, Bert and I doing the washing up in the early hours of the morning. Best of all, I got to meet Angela Rippon, then one of the most famous faces on television. She was absolutely charming and very pretty, though much more petite than you might have imagined after her famous high-kicking dance routine on the *Morecambe and Wise Show*. She and her husband lived in Tavistock, and she seemed to know Bert well, but then, who didn't in that part of the world.

●   ●   ●

Back at Westthorn, one of the major parts of my job was to focus on the blending and bottling activities within the complex, and to advise the company of ways to improve performance and overall quality. We had to ensure the consistent quality of raw materials, processes, and products, and there was also the little matter of a network of warehousing to take into account.

Some 650,000 barrels of whisky were held on five separate sites. This was nearly 80 million litres of alcohol, which, for a company that was not all that large, represented a very considerable investment. It was imperative that we got the maximum possible return on the investment in terms of sales of bottled whisky, but we also needed to cut down on operational and maturation losses wherever possible.

One of the biggest problems I encountered as QAM were the high level of operational losses in the blending and bottling operations at Westthorn. These were always above what I considered to be the industry average, so it was up to me to try to discover where and why these losses were occurring. Unfortunately, I had no authority to order any changes myself, I always had to work through the line managers, and they assured me that the levels of loss at Westthorn had always been this high; they maintained that they were unable to see where improvements could be made. After much investigation, we were forced to accept that this was the case.

Until I had been in Glasgow for about a year, the company has been able to use up duty-free samples which had been legally drawn to check on the quality of maturing spirit by bottling them in the 'duty-paid' section of the site. Although it was described as 'duty-paid', the area was technically 'duty-free' and was separate from the main bottling plant. Some years previously, Long John had bought out the old Aberdeen-based company of Gordon Graham Stewart, later Gordon Graham, who owned the Black Bottle brand of blended whisky. Long John, therefore, had two mainstream brands in the shape of Long John itself, and Black Bottle, which was then considered very much a secondary brand and received virtually no promotion. Black Bottle was produced from the duty-free samples at Westthorn, with all the component malts being tipped into one vat and all the grain whiskies into another. They were then mixed in the correct proportions. Because no duty had been paid on it, Black Bottle was a very profitable source of income for the company. The practice was then perfectly legal, and almost every whisky producer did the same with their duty-free samples, although after a while the Government clamped down on it, and it was made illegal in 1978. Interestingly, the operational losses in terms of percentages were far lower from the Black Bottle operation in the duty-paid section than they were from all the rest of the bottling, which took place in the main bottling hall. Nobody could ever come up with a reason for this. It was always just assumed that it must be due to two different sets of equipment.

Once duty-free bottling was discontinued, we had to decide

whether to continue producing Black Bottle. We also had a third blend in Islay Mist, which had been developed in a most memorable manner by Iain Hunter, the late owner of Laphroaig, who had handed over the distillery on his death to Bessie Williamson. The Margadale family owned a vast area of Islay even at the time when I was living there, and the then Lord Margadale had asked Iain to create a whisky for his son's coming of age party in 1928. The instructions were for a characterful whisky smooth enough for young ladies to drink, but strongly reminiscent of its Islay heritage. The result was a de-luxe blend which included Laphroaig, Glen Grant and The Glenlivet among its component malts. The final choice out of a number of trial blendings was down to Lord Margadale who had been warned by Iain that the one he was about to try might put him '...in a bit of a fog.' Lord Margadale duly tasted the whisky and after savouring it for a few moments, responded, 'No Iain...not a fog. A mist. Islay mist.' And so the name was born.

It was such a success that Iain decided to keep on blending it, and registered Islay Mist as a trademark. Long John inherited Islay Mist along with Laphroaig, and it continued to sell well. Overall, Black Bottle was the poorest performer of the three blends, but it was still a favourite in its native North-east, and market research suggested that it would be worth continuing to blend it. We came up with a blend formula, and it was decided to market it primarily in Scotland, with the intention of pushing it into England if it performed well at home. The Long John blend was very successful as an export whisky, but it wasn't so strong in the UK market, so promoting Black Bottle was not seriously going to interfere with its sales.

It was decided to establish a separate Black Bottle division at Westthorn, headed by John Campbell. John had previously worked for Bell's, and the profile of the blend was gradually raised through a substantial investment in advertising and promotion. The Black Bottle that is being so energetically marketed today is nothing like the blend of the 1970s, and I know quite a lot of people who prefer the old blend to the present one which now boasts all the Islays among its component malts.

Despite the fact that Whitbread had an expanding chain of tied pubs, restaurants, and the Thresher off-licence operation, each of these divisions had its own board of directors and was a trading company in its own right. They therefore felt no overwhelming loyalty to promote the Long John blend energetically, and if they could secure a better deal on supplies of a rival whisky, then they did so. It was company policy that all outlets should carry the brand, but there was no remit to promote it above any other, which seemed very strange. Not surprisingly, the Long John staff had expected sales of their whisky to increase dramatically once Whitbread took over the company, but this never happened and this created tensions within the organisation. Having bought Long John for £18m in 1975, Whitbread sold it in the late eighties for around £170m, so they didn't get a bad return on their investment, though at times it seemed that they could have done more to help themselves.

Whitbread placed a great deal of importance on the research and development side of the business. Once every quarter there was a QAMs' meeting in London, which provided an opportunity for discussion about developments in all the various divisions of the company. At one such meeting we were made aware of the potential dangers of NDMA, or nitrosamines, which had been found in German-brewed lager, and which tested as a carcinogen in rats under laboratory conditions. Admittedly, a human being would have had to consume vast amounts of alcohol each day in order to create a cancerous condition but it was still a matter of some concern. The situation was made known to the industry as a whole as there is a general policy of sharing such scientific information, even between rivals. Early indications suggested that if NDMA was present in lager, then it could also be present in whisky. After extensive tests, it was established that the occurrence of nitrosamines could largely be attributed to natural gas being used to dry barley in the malting kilns. As a result maltsters switched from direct drying with a naked gas heat source to indirect drying with gas being burnt to create hot air instead.

The fact that Whitbread operated on a comparatively large scale, was in contact with other major industry players all over the world, and did so much research and development work was very beneficial to Long John, and to the whisky industry in general. In addition to our own efforts, we co-operated quite closely with Chivas Bros on a number of projects. Pentlands Scotch Whisky Research Ltd also existed in order to carry out research work, having been formed in 1974 by a consortium of distillers.

To compete with some of the really major players in the whisky business it became necessary for Long John to increase efficiency, so it was decided to install a high-speed bottling line at Westhorn. We looked at models all over the world, and I had to swot up on whether an automatic 'de-palletiser' at the start of the production line would scratch the bottles, spoiling the presentation. Our objective was to cut the bottling line staff from around 20 to perhaps just three or four, with a target of filling 96,000 bottles of Long John blend each day. This was more than double our existing capability. Obviously, with such an increase in productivity and reduction in staff wages, our unit costs would fall dramatically. Eventually we installed a fully automated line, with a de-palletiser, an air cleaner, a 120-bottle filling-head, collection tables, two labellers, a wraparound carton mechanism, palletiser, shrink-wrap facility, and conveyor belts leading to fork-lift trucks. We spent a total of £1m on the bottling line project, but within two years the investment had been recovered, and the resultant annual saving was half a million pounds.

Unfortunately we ran into the problem that the line management of the bottling plant was not enthusiastic about the input from Whitbread's research and development staff, feeling, no doubt, that things had been managed perfectly well in the past. It made life difficult for me in that, as usual, I was stuck in the middle between the two factions, and was unable to do anything directly myself.

In terms of our home life, things were not going brilliantly either. Kay disliked the house, and was clearly pining for our happier days at Tormore. She had a naturally nervous disposition at the best of times, and Glasgow was certainly not making her feel better. She missed Speyside very much, and I have to admit that at times I felt the same. I was away from home quite a lot, whereas in the past I had always worked within a few minutes' walk of our house. We had school fees to pay, and there was also the financial pressure of a mortgage to contend with. For the first time in years, Kay was spending most of her days alone, with both children at school, and me at work, and she began to become depressed. While I was pleased to have been chosen for promotion within the company, I sometimes wondered why I had been selected for my new role. I can't say that I enjoyed the politics and pressures that are an inevitable part of working at somewhere like Westthorn, where there was a total staff of around 330 people. At that time it was the largest complex of its kind within the Scotch whisky industry, occupying a 100-acre site near Celtic's Parkhead stadium, complete with 22 warehouses, with a capacity of 500,000 barrels. The site had an asset value of around £60m, and contained £1 billion of maturing spirit stocks, taking duty into account. Not surprisingly, Westthorn boasted a security team of 22 men with Alsatian dogs and a system of 'magic eye' security beams. Despite this, a high perimeter fence and CCTV cameras, local lads still managed to get in and steal the wheel-trims from cars in the staff car park!

Chapter 11
Glasgow:
Complaints, Crashes
and Crooks

As QAM, I sometimes received letters of complaint from members of the public. One day I was passed a letter regarding Plymouth Gin. It was surprising the number of occasions on which letters of complaint were accompanied by a bottle of the product in question, usually at least three-quarters empty. It constantly amazed me just how long it took some people to detect that something was wrong with it. Bert Roberts kept a notebook of names and details of complaints received about Plymouth Gin, and in many cases there was a clear pattern of recurring complaints from the same individuals. I phoned Bert and mentioned the name of one of the complainants. He paused for a moment and then said, 'I wondered where his letter was this year. He always complains every January, and I thought that for once he was going to leave me in peace!' I told Bert that he was asking for two bottles to recompense him for the disappointment he had allegedly suffered. Bert responded, 'Cheeky sod! He just got one replaced in November.' We sent the customer one new bottle, along with a letter pointing out that we had replaced his last bottle only two months before Christmas and was it *that* replacement bottle which he had now returned? We never heard from him again.

On another occasion, however, one complaint did seem justified. Ian Coombs, our MD, was not a man to sit behind his desk when there were world markets to explore. He was very much a 'hands on' figure who could pop up in my part of the Long John operation with little or no notice. One day he arrived in my office hot off the plane from Spain, and presented me with an unopened 40-oz bottle of Long John whisky. 'How can you explain this, John?' he asked. I looked at the bottle carefully, and discovered that it contained a fly. My response of 'how unusual' probably wasn't what he wanted to hear, but I had no way of knowing how the insect had got in there. Ian told me that the offending bottle had been handed to him by the company's Spanish distributor as he got off his plane in Madrid. Not knowing quite how to respond, he had drawn himself up to his full height, and assuming all the dignity he could muster, said to the distributor, 'This is not a British fly, far less a Scottish fly. As we are in Spain, draw your own conclusions!'

● ● ●

South Africa was an extremely important export market for Long John International. The blend sold there was called Oldfield's Blue Label, which came in a Johnnie Walker-type square bottle, with a blue label. This was effectively Long John whisky, but with a slightly different malt to grain ratio. South Africa had very strict specifications for imported food and drink products in terms of chemical analysis, and anything which failed to meet their specifications was simply returned. Obviously, the implications of this were very serious for us. One day I received a phone call from a doctor of science at Stellenbosch University in South Africa, where many of the tests were carried out. He informed me that he had just analysed some samples of Blue Label, and they had been failed. I asked him what he suggested we should do, to which he replied that if we supplied him with some more of the whisky, he would re-test it and see whether the results differed.

'How much is required for the test?' I asked.

'Well, we use a small amount for the actual analysis, but due to the importance of the results to your company, we should perhaps err on the side of caution.'

'What, a bottle then?' I suggested.

'Umm, no…how about two cases?'

The penny dropped and the cases were duly despatched. This time the whisky passed.

In addition to my quality assurance role, I was subsequently appointed General Manager of Distilleries, with particular emphasis on the malt plants. This gave me the task of linking between the production director of Long John and the individual distillery managers, which made life more interesting for me. My Austin Maxi had been upgraded to a new silver Ford Granada, and the family was able to move to a more pleasant three-storey terraced house in the Pollockshields area of Glasgow. It seemed as though life was looking up again.

In my new role as GMD I got to spend time at Tormore and Glenugie, and in particular I enjoyed returning to Laphroaig. New maltings were built at Port Gordon and at Buckie, and in 1979 I attended the opening of the Port Gordon Maltings. This gave me a chance to see developments in malting technology, as well as visiting our distilleries while I was in the North-east. Unfortunately, on the way back to Glasgow, in very heavy rain on the M8, I was involved in an accident. A car coming in the opposite direction crossed the central reservation and hit my Granada. I was very shaken and bruised, although otherwise unhurt, but my car was an insurance write-off. Whitbread supplied me with an Alfa Romeo Alfetta as a replacement, and soon after taking delivery of that, someone drove into the rear of it as I waited in a line of traffic. Unbelievably, on the first day I got the car back after repairs, a bus rammed into the front of it in Glasgow city centre. Kay had always viewed cars with some suspicion, partly as a result of having failed her driving test three times and given up on the notion of passing it. My three accidents in the space of a month did nothing to change her views. They didn't do much for me either, but I had to accept that this was one of the hazards of city life, and just carry on driving, keeping an even sharper eye out for potential dangers than I had in the past.

Westthorn was quite a low-lying site, with the River Clyde flowing close to the southern side of the complex. The old Westthorn Farm had been known to flood in the past, so Long John had built substantial defences into the river banks. On one occasion, however, when it had rained non-stop for what seemed like weeks, the water level rose so high that it breached the berm and flooded the site on a massive scale. The water was up to 15 feet deep in some of the warehouses, which meant that after a very lengthy clearing up operation, we had to test every single cask, just in case the filthy flood water had contaminated any of them. Given the scale of Westthorn, this was a daunting task, and we found ourselves working virtually round the clock to get the job done. Needless to say, as QAM, it was up to me to organise and supervise the work. In addition to all the casks filled with spirit which were warehoused on the site, we also had some 60,000 empty barrels stacked in the open. These were on site awaiting filling at Westthorn with new spirit from Strathclyde Grain Distillery. During the flood, many of these empty barrels floated away down the Clyde, and could be seen from the Broomielaw, bobbing their way towards the open sea.

One of the most dramatic events during my time at Westthorn occurred in November 1981, when I was summoned early one Friday morning by Ian Coombs to the company's head office in Franborough House, Bothwell Street. There I found Ian and Charles Strickland, from what would nowadays be called Whitbread's Human Resource Department. Ian Coombs was looking very grave, and said to me, 'John, I'll come straight to the point. There has been a degree of impropriety at Westthorn, as a result of which we have suspended the general manager, the deputy general manager, the bottling hall manager, and the bottling hall engineer. Do you know why we've done this?'

I was absolutely astonished, and could only shake my head. I hadn't a clue what he was talking about. I asked him to explain what was happening, and he told me that there had been serious misappropriation of whisky from Westthorn, and that customs and excise were about to become involved. He wanted to know if there was anything I could contribute to the enquiry. I told him that there wasn't, that I was totally in the dark about the whole matter. He clearly believed me, because he proceeded to appoint me acting general manager with immediate effect. He told me to return to Westthorn, where I was to read a prepared statement to the assembled workforce in the canteen.

I was finding it quite difficult to believe what was happening. Here I was, just beginning to get to grips with my quality assurance role and responsibilities as GDM, when suddenly I was in charge of the most important site in the whole of Long John International, and in the most difficult of circumstances imaginable. Back at Westthorn, I not only had to address the staff, but also had to put in place an entirely new management team before lunch. Facing more than 300 staff and telling them of the suspensions was a traumatic business. They were as astonished as I had been, and very little work was done that day. People stood around in little huddles, discussing and speculating.

I took the view that we had to put together a team which had immediate credibility with staff at all levels, as well as with the customs and excise service. We also had to co-operate with their special investigation branch, which moved into Westthorn immediately and began to work systematically through the offices of the suspended employees. To make the day even worse, I was summoned by the customs' team to the general manager's office during the afternoon. There I was shown a couple of guns and some ammunition, and was asked if I knew that these items were on the premises. As with most events of that day, all I could do was shake my head and look astonished.

Unbeknown to me, there had been a low-key undercover operation in progress at the site for some time, instigated by Jim McGivern, an ex-Whitbread personnel director from County Antrim in Northern Ireland. This had unearthed the thefts of whisky, and led to the suspensions. There was a cemetery just beyond the perimeter fence on one side of the Westthorn site. It transpired that in addition to the whisky which had been going missing from the site proper, some had probably disappeared from tankers delivering spirit from Strathclyde to the filling store. Containers of the stuff had been thrown over the fence – and therefore over the 'magic eye' security beam – into the cemetery for collection later.

I was told by Jim not to answer my house door or the phone that weekend, as he was concerned for my safety and that of my family. I think the discovery of the guns had unnerved him a bit, which was perhaps something to do with coming from County Antrim. He was not alone in being unnerved. I went home on Friday evening feeling exhausted and terrified, not knowing how I was going to broach the subject with Kay. I sat her down and chatted about my day in general as casually as I could, before finally mentioning the guns and Jim's concerns. More than ever that evening we harked back to our previous rural existence, where the wildlife was natural, rather than of the man-made variety.

Nothing untoward happened over the weekend, and by Monday I was feeling slightly more on top of the situation. We continued to work on the management changes, which included bringing Mike Walker into the quality assurance role, while John Sloan was made production accountant and engineer. We promoted a more open style of management, and at the same time tightened up on reporting procedures, so that hopefully the same sort of situation could not occur again in the future. We made it known that anyone on the shop floor would be considered for promotion to staff positions, should they be good enough. All in all, we carried out a radical shake-up of the whole management structure at Westthorn. Clearly, it had been needed.

It transpired that a sizeable quantity of whisky had gone missing, so Long John had to pay customs and excise a large sum of money by way of recompense. Due to Ian Coombs' prompt and efficient response to the situation, however, the amount paid was a lot less than it might have been. The fact that certain officers of HM Customs & Excise were allegedly involved in the thefts also served as mitigation as far as the company was concerned. The complicity of some excise officers partly explained why it had been so difficult to detect the fraud, which was actually very elaborate and sophisticated. This was no copper tube down the wellington boot operation! Several of the people at management level who had been responsible for organising the scam had been with the company when the Westthorn plant was first developed, so the high level of production losses had been evident from the start. There were therefore less grounds for suspicion than would have been the case if losses had suddenly risen. Not too surprisingly, following the dismissal of the staff in question and a period of reorganisation, production losses fell significantly.

After all the stresses and traumas of the suspensions, we only had a few weeks of calm before the next major crisis. At that time, wages for the hourly-paid staff were still given in cash. On the last day that Westthorn was working before the Christmas break I glanced out of my office window around 11am and saw the Group 4 security van which was due to bring our Christmas wages. Unfortunately, by the time it arrived it was empty, having been held up by a group of men with sawn-off shotguns just along the road. Not only did our money disappear, but also that destined for the nearby bus depot at Parkhead. In total, around £60,000 was taken in the robbery, and some of the money eventually surfaced in Dorset. I was faced with the delicate problem of telling the workers that there was no cash with which to pay them before Christmas. Addressing them to reveal the suspensions had been a picnic compared to what now lay ahead!

We summoned the staff together in the canteen and I duly told them what had happened, though their predictable anger was not directed at me or the company, because everyone appreciated that it was not our fault. I softened the blow by saying that Long John would provide free lunch and beer while the cashiers sorted out a new wages run from the bank. This was the cue for a serious party to develop, with someone fetching a record player, while those who fancied themselves as singers took to the floor and serenaded their fellow workers. I think everyone was quite disappointed when the next batch of wages turned up at around four o'clock in the afternoon and the party had to break up. A lot of the women from the bottling hall had been planning to spend the afternoon Christmas shopping, and I dread to think what they ended up buying!

I was sitting in my office after the last staff had left, musing on the strange and eventful end to the year when our new security manager, Roy Standring, an ex-major in the military police, knocked on the door, and inquired whether I wanted even more bad news. 'You remember that container load of twelve-year-old deluxe Long John we sent off to Spain at the start of the week?' With a sinking feeling already beginning in my stomach, I replied, 'You mean the one that was to be there before Christmas?' 'That's the one', responded Roy, '…well, it's gone missing.' Nothing I could say would persuade him to admit that this was a joke in very poor taste. Apparently the truck had got no further than the lorry park at Birkenhead, on Merseyside. The loss of one container may not seem like a massive problem, but it had 1,200 cases of whisky in it, or 14,400 bottles. I remember thinking that it would be difficult to imagine what else could have gone wrong during the six weeks since I'd had my new job! The container was discovered a few days later, but not surprisingly it turned out to be empty. Some months into the New Year quite a few of the bottles of Long John deluxe were found to be on sale in some of the back-street dives of Liverpool, but I never did learn if the perpetrators were caught.

I enjoyed the challenges of work, and I learnt a lot more about business than I ever would if I had remained a distillery manager, but there was no escaping the fact that I felt my life was heading in a way I had never really wanted it to, and that my marriage and other family relationships were suffering as a result. I had to spend a couple of days away from Glasgow most weeks, and there were visitors from all over the world to entertain when they came to Westthorn. Work was certainly not confined to a nine to five routine.

I was, at least, fortunate in having a first-class secretary in May MacTavish, who was only in her early twenties, but possessed maturity beyond her years. She was excellent at organising my working life and fielding difficult phone calls and visitors. She also had a great sense of humour, which helped me a lot during what were quite difficult times. I was fortunate in having extremely good people within Long John who worked as my right hand men and women, and indeed I had always been lucky with my staff at that level. In my days at Tormore there had been Fiona and Lesley, and Rachel and Betty at Laphroaig. These were all people for whom I had a great deal of respect.

Between 1981 and 1983 a number of major appointments were made to the Long John International board. A new MD was appointed when Ian Coombs moved on, and a new production director replaced that great character Duncan McGregor. There were also changes in the secretariat of the company and at finance director

level. The new MD was very much sales and marketing orientated. He
was an extremely commercially-minded man by the name of Tony
Derry, who had been a successful sales and marketing director of Bell's,
before that company had been taken over by Guinness in 1985. He had
worked with Whyte & Mackay for a short time before joining Long
John, where his remit was to shake things up a bit, and he certainly did
that. We didn't always see eye to eye on a professional level, and we
disagreed about a good many matters. One example was regarding
programmes for bottling, where we would be instructed to abandon
one job at very short notice in order to do another where it was felt
there might be greater personal and customer satisfaction. This was all
very well in one respect, but obviously contributed to higher unit
costs. It was classic 'Catch 22' stuff.

I was now very unhappy in my personal and professional life,
and my health was suffering as a result. After a great deal of careful
consideration I resigned from Long John International at the end of
1984. Kay and I decided to move back to the countryside, and bought
a property incorporating a general store in the little village of
Auchencairn, on the shores of the Solway Firth in Kirkudbrightshire.
There was a rare and very different breed of people in that particular
corner of Scotland, known as 'Gallowa' Irish'. They were warm, yet
fiery! We hoped that our move would bring us all closer together as a
family, but it didn't work out that way, and Kay ended up needing
medical treatment for depression. We stayed in Aucherncairn for a year,
but another change of direction was in the offing.

Chapter 12
Campbeltown:
Wright or Wrong?

The happiest and most fulfilling times of my working life had always been when I was running my own distilleries, and with this in mind I began to look for a job back in distillery management. I was extremely fortunate to be appointed manager of J&A Mitchell & Co's Springbank Distillery in Campbeltown during the autumn of 1986. I took over from Roy Allan, who had been there for 40 years before retiring, though he was retained by the company on a part-time consultancy basis.

Although I began work at Springbank in November 1986, it wasn't until the following summer that we sold our Solway property, so there was really no alternative but for Kay and the children to stay down there during that time. In effect I was taking two or three steps backwards in terms of my experience, but I was very enthusiastic about the prospect of being at the heart of 'real' distilling once more. My salary was obviously a lot smaller than it had been with Long John, but I felt there was cause for optimism in that I was back doing what I really enjoyed, I was away from the city, and the whisky industry was coming out of recession.

I was appointed to my new job by Hedley Wright, who was

MD of J&A Mitchell & Co, and when I went for my interview with him I already knew the man by reputation. I had also met him briefly some years earlier at the centenary of the MDA at Aviemore in 1974. He was a tall, red-haired, red-bearded man who wore a kilt on formal occasions, carried himself well, and looked not unlike King George V. He would certainly not be missed in a crowd.

I had an informal interview with him one Saturday afternoon in September when Scotland were playing rugby against Japan at Murrayfield. I remember thinking that there seemed to be something about me and interviews while Scottish rugby matches were in progress. It had been during a Scotland match that Duncan McGregor had first asked me if I would like to be manager of Laphroaig. We met at Cadenhead's whisky shop on the Canongate in Edinburgh, although I didn't realise at the time that Cadenhead's was a subsidiary company of J&A Mitchell & Co. We crossed the Royal Mile to a little café, where we discussed the manager's job at Springbank and Hedley was generous enough to describe my CV as 'immaculate'. I asked him what budgetary controls were employed by the company. 'Budgetary controls, Mr McDougall?', he queried, raising his eyebrows. 'The only budgetary controls we operate are that we don't spend any money.' That fact became very obvious once I took up my appointment. The distilling industry has always gone through boom and bust on a cyclical basis, and it was going through one such recessionary period at that time, so it wasn't unreasonable that very little money had been spent on Springbank for a number of years.

It was like going back to Laphroaig, only a stage further back, because Springbank distillery was in an extremely poor state of repair. It consisted of the most ramshackle collection of whitewashed stone buildings one was ever likely to encounter. The previous manager had stored hundreds of empty casks on the ground floor of the disused malt barns, but these were next to useless because they had been saturated as the roof had rotted through. Large areas of the yard were also filled with empty casks, and there was a surfeit of these in the industry at the time because of low production levels of new spirit due to the recession. What Springbank did have, however, was a very good product, along with a small bottling facility. Apart from Glenfiddich, it was the only distillery in Scotland that bottled on the premises. Another notable feature of Springbank was that it operated a sequence of three stills, rather than the usual two. The whisky is sometimes mistakenly described as 'triple-distilled', but in practice it is more a case of two-and-a-half-times distillation. When I went there the distillery had not produced new spirit for several years, and there was no plan to do so during 1986/87. What I had moved back to was a silent distillery which had two or three male staff, eight female staff, plus an old joiner called Peter MacSporran, who came 'with the fittings'.

Because of the state of our family finances, I lived in a caravan for my first winter in Campbeltown. This was unquestionably the coldest period of my life. When I went to bed I'd reluctantly turn off the Calor gas heater, so that I wouldn't be suffocated, and I slept in a duffle-coat, scarf and sometimes even gloves. Being gassed seemed like a better alternative at times. Because Campbeltown was so exposed to gales, steel cables were stretched across the top of the caravan and anchored into concrete blocks in the ground. I used to worry that the caravan would be picked up by the wind during the night and carried out into Campbeltown Loch, and that I would wake up floating in the Atlantic. The caravan rental was only £12 per week, however, which made the discomforts worthwhile in the longer term. In February I was allocated a council flat, and the night before I moved in, a particularly wild storm blew up, causing the caravan to lurch alarmingly in spite of its anchors. Not daring to go to bed, I sat up, fully dressed. Around four o'clock in the morning I could stand it no longer and I decided to pack and leave there and then. It was just as well that I did because the caravan had moved so far that it was now very close up to a wall, and I could only just squeeze out of the door. I drove the car into a sheltered corner of the site, and stayed there for a few hours before driving to the flat in town. The luxury of being able to sleep without wearing a duffle coat and without worrying about waking up in the sea was quite wonderful.

Campbeltown is situated near the end of the long and remote Kintyre peninsula, and the place seemed to be caught in a time warp in some respects, particularly in terms of social and structural development. The people were much more introverted and difficult to get to know than they had been on Islay. It was generally recognised that if they didn't know about your business then they would either work hard to find out, or simply make it up. The town was perhaps 50 years behind everywhere else, though it had a certain charm. It was 140 miles south-west of Glasgow, which meant that in some ways it was more cut off than Islay. Moving to Glasgow from Tormore had been a culture shock, and now I was experiencing a culture shock in reverse. The Kintyre peninsula is extremely beautiful, and has a kind of grandeur all its own; it's never the same two days running, and the sea is always close at hand. It could very easily be an island, and only the one-mile-wide isthmus between East Loch Tarbert and West Loch Tarbert stops it from being one.

When I arrived in Campbeltown to start work I felt at first that I had gone to the most God-forsaken spot in Scotland. The town seemed to be full of pubs and churches, with the pubs having got busier over the years, while the churches had got quieter. Campbeltown had been established by one of the Dukes of Argyll during the early 17th century, and had developed as an industrial centre, partly because Campbeltown Loch provided an excellent natural harbour. At one time the town had a foundry, an engineering works, coppersmithing operations, and of course lots of distilleries, as well as the herring trade, which was a major local employer. There was even a small railway which ran along the seafront and out to Machrihanish, and there was a coal mine at Drumlemble which provided fuel not only for domestic use, but also to fire the stills in all the distilleries. There was also a shipbuilding yard, which worked until quite recently, at one time making vessels of several thousand tons displacement, rather than just the small fishing boats it built latterly. When I went to Campbeltown there were still more than 30 fishing boats based there, but I believe there are now less than 20.

One of the mainstays of the local economy at that time was the Jaeger clothes factory, which employed around 300 people. The creamery was also a significant employer, as was RAF Machrihanish, a NATO base which put a lot of money into the economy. There was a resident RAF and US navy presence, in addition to which the German, Dutch and other foreign services regularly came over on NATO exercises.

At the turn of the century Campbeltown had about 30 distilleries in operation, and was called 'whisky city' by the great Victorian whisky chronicler, Alfred Barnard, when he visited it in 1886. By the time I went there, however, the town had only two distilleries left. Of those, Springbank was in occasional production, and Glen Scotia was intact, but silent. The town is open to Atlantic gales and as a result is very windswept. The brine sweeps through the town, giving the Campbeltown whiskies a distinctive flavouring of salt. During the 1920s the ever-enlarging DCL bought up many of the struggling, independent distilleries and then closed them in order to rationalise the production of whisky in Scotland. (They also took the roofs off them, in order to avoid having to pay rates.) The Mitchell family had owned both Springbank and Rieclachan distilleries, the latter of which was in production from the 1820s until 1934.

Unlike all the other malt distilleries with which I had previously been associated, Springbank is situated in the middle of the town. It is located up a close known as Well Close, behind the Springbank Gospel Hall. It amused me that drink was seen as the root of all evil by people such as the Gospel Hall congregation, yet here they were, meeting right next to one of the last remaining distilleries in the town, and surrounded by warehouses of spirit. The Lowland Church, with its high clock tower, is also clearly visible from the distillery, and this church was reputedly built with distillers' money. In fact, Campbeltown is very well supplied with places of worship, several of which owe their existence to whisky-makers. Perhaps they felt the need to try to secure places in Heaven by doing this, after making money in ways which they thought God would not have liked. After his visit, Alfred Barnard wrote:

Sunday in Campbeltown is carried to its Jewish length, and is quite a day of gloom and penance. The churches and chapels, which are scattered all over the town, are crowded with well dressed and staid looking people, and everybody carries a pious look on that day. Neither music nor whistling is allowed in either the houses or streets, and the landlady of the hotel was quite shocked at our proposing to play some sacred music on the piano. We might have expected this, as it is said that there are nearly as many places of worship as distilleries in the town.

Hedley Wright was an eccentric, an academic, and a man who had never really wanted to join the family company. He had only come into the business after his father died, and he had hoped to have retired by the time he was in his forties. He gave me the impression of being determined and reclusive. He was not a great communicator although I believe he had spent time as a university lecturer, having gained a geology degree from Cambridge. He was the great, great grandson of the distillery's founder, Archibald Mitchell and had even been to Antarctica as part of a British survey team in his youth. He told me once that during the week each of the national contingents worked in isolation from one another, maintaining a very literal Cold War. At the weekends, however, the British and Americans would turn up on Saturday at the entrance to the Soviet camp, and make formal complaints about their presence in the region. The Soviets would respond with some rhetoric about the glories of the Soviet Socialist Republics and the communist state, before inviting them all in and abandoning all protocol in a haze of vodka, bourbon and Scotch whisky. The next weekend, the Soviets would arrive at the American camp to complain about *their* presence, and the whole thing would happen all over again.

Hedley's determination had probably been a positive force in helping to keep Springbank alive during the period of difficulty from the late seventies until the early nineties. The company was in dire financial straits, and a lot of business had evaporated by the seventies. Previously, Mitchell's had fulfilled fillings contracts for other companies in the industry, and had built up a good rapport with some of the big distillers. Hedley Wright's father, Gordon, had enjoyed a very good working relationship with most of the industry, and especially with DCL, but Hedley had had greater difficulty. With the onset of economic recession, meant that Springbank lost out on lots of business. To his credit, Hedley could have sold up quite easily during these difficult times as there were plenty of interested potential buyers, due to Springbank's excellent reputation as a single malt. Hedley told me once that, on average, he received around one offer every month regarding the sale of the company. He chose to soldier on, however, and keep the firm in the family. In many ways, Hedley was a throwback to a previous era, but he embraced new technology with some enthusiasm, on one occasion buying second-hand Apple Mac computers from the United States via mail order!

Once the new fillings business began to dry up, it was obvious that there had to be a major push in bottled sales of the single malt. Hedley had had the foresight to purchase the oldest independent bottling company in the industry, William Cadenhead of Aberdeen, which meant that not only was Springbank bottled in the tiny hands-on facility at the distillery, but Cadenhead's products were also bottled there. The acquisition of Cadenhead's had been a shrewd business move, as was the previous decision to house a bottling facility at the distillery: when the distillery wasn't producing spirit, it was the little bottling plant that paid to keep the rest of the operation afloat.

When I went to Campbeltown, Bill Thomson was the export sales manager for Springbank, and MD of Cadenhead. The group of companies owned by Mitchell & Co also included Eaglesome, which was an old-established grocer and wine and spirit merchant in Campbeltown. Hedley described Eaglesome's as 'a Campbeltown Fortnum & Mason', and if you really stretched your imagination then you could almost see what he was getting at…well, almost. It was actually just a small shop, but it did provide a shop window in the town for the company's products. Eaglesome operated not just as a retail outlet, but also as wholesaler for the Springbank products in the UK, and I was subsequently appointed MD of Eaglesome. Along with Eaglesome, Hedley had also bought the Kintyre and Kinloch bars, which were situated on a prime corner site between Longrow South and Main Street. The previous MD of Eaglesome, John Galt, had talked Hedley into turning the bars into a discotheque called 'Splash'. It became popular with servicemen from RAF Machrihanish, and for a time 'Splash' was the place to go. The overall business clearly needed an injection of capital, however, and we decided to sell 'Splash', in order to release some money to spend on the distillery. The sale was achieved before the next economic downturn really hit home, and we were fortunate to have been able to sell it when we did. This was probably the turning point for starting to get the whole business back onto a sounder footing.

Hedley was often away from Campbeltown, spending a lot of his life in Edinburgh and London. The winter of 1987/88 was a difficult time, with very little bottling work and few orders to fill, and Hedley was away for six weeks on a foreign skiing holiday. Skiing was one of his great passions, and something which he had taken up as a young man when it was still an exclusive sport.

This was the sort of management culture of the company, which was, and almost certainly remains, unique within the Scotch whisky industry. In a way I quite admired him, as he was doing his best, as he saw it, to keep the company going for the family shareholders. He was, indeed, the largest individual shareholder in what still is the oldest family-owned distillery in Scotland.

The Machrihanish airbase presented us with a lucrative sales opportunity, as Bill Thomson had set up an operation selling cases of duty-free Springbank to visiting forces through one of the RAF sergeants. In order to do this legally, we had to deliver the orders right onto the aircraft. We used to drive our cars down the runway and stow the whisky on board huge USAF Galaxies and Starlifters; the sort of aircraft that were big enough to carry helicopters in their holds. The Machrihanish base was gradually wound down, and in 1996 it closed altogether, which was quite a blow for the economy of Kintyre. The shipyard also finally ceased trading, and with the contraction of the fishing industry and bad times in farming, things became quite bleak. Because of its isolated location, it was always difficult to get business people to invest much money in Campbeltown.

Chapter 13
Campbeltown:
Company Craic

Bill Thomson was a born salesman, a character with lots of patter. For many years he had run his own business in Belgium, before joining Mitchell's. He enjoyed life to the full, and I recall one occasion when he was to go to France, then on to Belgium and Switzerland. France was an important market for the Scotch whisky industry in general, but it was a very significant one for Springbank. Bill was due to meet a contact in Geneva who had ambitions to be our Swiss distributor, and Bill was to fly from Paris to Geneva to meet him. When the contact phoned us to say that Bill hadn't turned up we began to get concerned, especially as he couldn't be traced in France either. After two days, we decided to get in touch with the police and ask them what we should do, imagining that Bill had been attacked or taken ill. Finally, we phoned his wife to inform her about our concerns, only to be told, 'Oh he's here…do you want to speak to him?' Well, yes, we did. It turned out that Bill had never left Campbeltown. Somewhat disillusioned with Springbank, it appeared that he had simply decided to have an unofficial break from work.

Not long after this, we were conducting our annual stocktaking of bottling and 'dry goods' materials, which were Bill's responsibility.

The auditor from Glasgow asked Bill for the value of the dry goods stock, to which he replied, 'Could be a pound, could be a hundred thousand pounds. Take your pick, sunshine. Call it anything you like, because tomorrow I'm off.' We all just assumed this was Bill having a bad day, and thought no more about it, but when it got to lunchtime the following day he suddenly said, 'Well that's me away, Bye then,' and left, never to return. Bill's had worked enthusiastically and developed new markets at Springbank (although in times of recession he had operated a very generous case price policy) so his disillusionment was a little difficult to fathom.

When I first went to Springbank in 1986 there was a resident excise officer by the name of Steve Etough, who despite being no more than five-foot-six, insisted that he had played rugby as second-row forward at the highest level. Being no stranger to the game myself, I knew that someone of five-foot-six would *not* have made a very effective lock forward. Steve's superior was a little Ulsterman called Billy Campbell and one of the great pleasures of Springbank at that time was watching him barge into Hedley's office, shouting and bawling about some minor transgression. Hedley had no alternative but to at least hear Billy out, as he did represent the law. Eventually Billy would storm out of Hedley's room and write a letter complaining about whatever was wrong, which would duly be passed on to me. I would be asked to reply, and a copy would go to Hedley, and the whole thing just went round in circles. Happily, I was soon to be pre-occupied with more pressing responsibilities.

During 1987/88 we conducted a distilling season, albeit in fairly difficult circumstances. The plant had fallen into quite a state of disrepair while the distillery had been silent, and before we could begin to make whisky again, we had to get Peter McSporran to construct wooden 'bridges' and install handrails in order to make the place a bit safer. It was almost a miracle that we ever got it working again, and it took quite a bit of ingenuity at times, but the first spirit flowed in late 1987, and very decent stuff it was too. Even the yields weren't too bad, considering how long the plant had been closed. Five of the six washbacks were useable, though one leaked quite badly until we plugged the gaps from the outside with cement. I was thrilled to get the distillery up and running again, but I knew that we needed to spend some money upgrading it to comply with various health and safety regulations. One task was ensuring that malt being delivered by lorry flowed smoothly off the top of the intake elevator onto the conveyor, before being deposited in the malt storage bins, which were situated in part of the rotten malt barn buildings. Hedley had had the foresight to retain the stillman, Hector Gatt, even when the distillery was silent, and this proved to be a very shrewd move, as Hector was probably the finest stillman I ever worked with.

We did spend some money on the plant, which enabled us to re-floor the tun room where the wooden slats had almost rotted through, and we put in new stainless steel outlet pipes from the washbacks to the wash pump. The tun room and the stillhouse were both painted from top to bottom, and the stills themselves were cleaned. We also had the funds to repair various roofs, and to tidy up the bottling hall.

In August 1987 Kay and the children came to join me in Campbeltown, as the house by the Solway had finally been sold. Unfortunately this meant another change of school, and Jonathan, aged 17, had to leave Kirkudbright Academy where he had played badminton against an extremely competitive boy by the name of David Coulthard. I hoped that now we were together as a family once more, things would get better, but the four of us were living in a small flat in Campbeltown which was not much bigger than our first Glasgow home, and pressures and tensions arose much as before. In June 1988, however, we were able to move into a fairly spacious apartment owned by Mitchell's in Longrow, which improved matters in the short term. We could look out of the windows of the flat and see the distillery, a bit like at Laphroaig and Tormore, except that here we were living above a furniture shop, a pub, an ice cream parlour and a Chinese take-away. Hardly the romantic, mystical image of distilling that the Speyside Whisky Trail conjures up! At Tormore it had not been unknown for one of the distillery workers to bring a freshly-caught trout from the Spey into the canteen and cook it during a break in his shift: at Springbank they would bring in chicken chow mein to heat up.

By early 1988 the company finances were looking healthier, and we were in a position to employ a trainee distillery manager. Denzil Meyrick had been a policeman in Glasgow and was recommended to us for the job by Lilian Campbell. Lilian was the old clerkess at Springbank, and something of a power behind Hedley's throne. Her husband was employed as the distillery security officer, and he too had formerly been a policeman, with the old Argyll force. When Bill Thomson walked out we no longer had a sales manager, and it fell to me, helped by Denzil, to maintain relations with existing customers and try to get new ones. We installed a fax machine, and with the aid of this I kept in contact with clients throughout the world. We were actually able to increase sales quite significantly, though we were obviously helped by the fact that the whisky industry was emerging from recession, and the situation was improving for everyone. I began to develop a real interest in sales, and I also began to buy casks of whisky as an investment. I asked Hedley's advice about purchasing new fillings of Springbank with some money I had acquired from a stock market speculation some years previously, and he replied that while profits could never be guaranteed, he had never known anyone to lose their 'stake money' on a whisky investment, provided you can afford to hold onto it for long enough. Early in 1989 I bought a few casks of new Springbank, and continued to build up my holding from time to time until I left the company in 1996, by which time I had spent a total of around £20,000 on new fillings.

Springbank was originally a farm, owned by the Mitchell

family, who ran a 'bootleg' still as a sideline, as was so often the case. The legal distillery was built in 1828, and members of the family always tried to maintain traditional methods as far as possible, though that was made more difficult when the maltings were closed for some 20 years. We ran a project in 1990 to bring the maltings back into production, using local labour, and I was very proud to be part of that. We took advice from a consultant about the best way of renewing the maltings building, which was basically a semi-derelict three-storey stone construction. The result was that we decided to rebuild the maltings in traditional style using our own labour, which included Peter MacSporran, who was wont, after a dram or two, to describe his hands as, 'precision hand tools'. His face would get progressively redder with each drink, and he would wax lyrical about the necessity of preserving these delicate objects so that he could continue to carry out the type of work for which he claimed to be renowned. Peter was also a great storyteller, and he reckoned to have been a pilot, a deep-sea diver and an elephant trainer; usually in that order.

On one occasion we had a retirement party for Ranald Watson, one of the Springbank staff, and Peter MacSporran was one of two other men retiring under the auspices of the same party. The event took place in the function room of Campbeltown's White Hart Hotel, and I made the usual speeches about the merits of the three retirees, during which I couldn't help but feel that I didn't quite have the full attention of the assembled guests. This turned out to be because they were all eyeing up the limited quantity of free drink which was on a large table at the opposite side of the room. The moment I had finished speaking there was a mad dash for the table, but I thought it was considerate that several of the women from the bottling hall were carrying handfuls of extra drinks back to their friends. I said as much to one, only to be greeted with a look of pure pity, and the comment, 'What friends? These are for me.' Peter's face got very red that night, and the stories flowed faster than the drinks. Well, almost.

The work on the maltings took 18 months, and in April 1992 the first malt was produced. Springbank was now the only distillery in Scotland that handled every aspect of production on site. Grant's of Glenfiddich might take issue with that, and they do make their own malt, but they do so at Balvenie, rather than at Glenfiddich itself. Most of the other distilleries that do their own malting tend to do so now for 'window dressing' purposes, in order to please visitors and allow claims of traditional methods to be made. Laphroaig is perhaps an exception to this, although it only makes 30 percent of its malt requirement. For us, the real justification for operating our own maltings was so that we could produce malt to the exact specification we wanted. We had control over the whole operation.

The briny, sweet Campbeltown-style of whiskies had gone out of fashion as standardisation and rationalisation took a grip on the industry, but in a small company like Mitchell's the arguments in favour of standardisation could be ignored by a figure like Hedley. The result was that Springbank made a more characterful whisky than most distilleries, and by producing our own malt we were helping to ensure that this state of affairs would continue in an age when a lot of whisky was racing down the road towards blandness. The proof of the pudding will be in the eating, or rather drinking, when the spirit made using the company's own malt is released as a single malt at 12 years of age. Springbank is only ever sold as a single malt, it never goes for blending, and the public has become progressively more interested in drinking single malts during the past couple of decades. Something of a 'real whisky' movement, parallel to the 'real ale' movement, has developed, and distillers and their marketing people have begun to exploit this move back to whisky's roots.

Springbank took the ultimate step back to whisky's roots by producing what was recognised as the world's first organic malt whisky of modern times. This was distilled by us using organically-grown barley for a Welsh dairy farmer and renowned cheesemaker by the name of John Savage Ondswedder. We even painted the cask ends green and stencilled 'Organic' onto them so that we could easily identify the casks in the warehouse.

The re-introduction of Springbank's maltings helped to secure the future of the distillery's other malt, Longrow, which was named after a distillery that had stood on a site adjoining Springbank. In my time at Springbank we distilled Longrow just once per season, making around 55 hogsheads of spirit, which meant that we effectively rationed it. Longrow is very heavily peated whisky, and is made using only peat in the drying process in the maltings. It is also quite oily, and is closer to an Islay whisky than to most mainland malts. It really hits you with its pungency, and is much sought after by collectors and true aficionados. If anything, it has become more robust since the re-opening of the maltings. We certainly didn't agree about everything, but I was in agreement with Hedley Wright about the use of traditional methods to produce really good, individualistic whisky. Longrow is distilled in a different way to Springbank, although the same distillation equipment is used, and the method employed brings out a greater degree of oiliness.

I was thoroughly enjoying having a hands-on role in a small company, and the job satisfaction level for me was very high. On the domestic front, however, things were getting no better, and after much soul-searching through the early months of 1989, Kay and I decided to split up. She went back to her mother, who was now living near Stirling, taking Louise with her. Jonathan stayed with me for a time before starting his own career, which began at Springbank, after which he moved to the central belt and employment with a local authority.

After Kay's departure, Hedley decided that it would be good for me if I accompanied him to the VINEXPO trade fair in Bordeaux, where Springbank was to have a trade stand. The job of attending the show fell to Hedley because Bill Thomson had left the company. For reasons of his own that I never did work out, it was arranged we would travel independently to Portsmouth, where we were to meet up at the ferry terminal prior to the long sailing to Le Havre. As a boy in Fife I had travelled regularly on the old Forth ferry which pre-dated the construction of the Forth Road Bridge, then graduated to the Islay ferry, and now I was on one of the largest car ferries in existence. As we left Portsmouth we sailed past the navy's new HMS *Campbeltown*, which was being commissioned at the time. It was interesting to see this ship, which had been written about at some length in the *Campbeltown Courier* before it went into service and paid its first visit to Campbeltown. A few years later, HMS *Campbeltown* came 'home' and we received a ship-to-shore phone call from Prince Andrew, no less, asking if it would be possible for him and some fellow officers from the ship to tour Springbank. Needless to say, we were delighted to show them round.

Hedley and I arrived in Le Havre around 9pm, and set off in Hedley's Vauxhall Cavalier for the drive to Bordeaux. Of course, he could have driven a Mercedes or a Jaguar, but it was in keeping with his character that he chose not to follow that 'herd'. Hedley's Cavalier had originally been red, but because he had a strict policy of refusing to wash his cars at any time, I had to take this on trust. I was told by somebody in Campbeltown that on one occasion the vehicle had been at the local garage for a service, and when he collected it, Hedley had complained very loudly and at great length because they had presumed to wash it for him.

Hedley decided that I should navigate, and as we left the docks I saw a sign which indicated Bordeaux was to the left. I told Hedley, who duly turned left, but instead of leaving Le Havre we found ourselves back at the dock gates a few minutes later. It was only when we went past for the third time that I realised the sign actually said 'Bordeaux Hotel'. Hedley was not best pleased, and decided to navigate the rest of the way himself. We arrived in Bordeaux just as dawn was breaking, and booked into our hotel.

Everything had been reserved in the name of Bill Thomson, and Hedley decided that it would be best if I 'became' Bill for the duration of our visit, saying that it would save all the confusion of changing the name to McDougall in the hotel and at the exhibition centre. We duly booked into our separate rooms. Bill was not a man to deny himself the little luxuries of life, and I thought there was going to be an immediate dividend for me when I discovered that Bill had booked himself a suite. There was an ante-room off the large bedroom, a fine bathroom, and even a writing room, and I decided that as I was now 'Bill Thomson' I wouldn't mention the standard of my accommodation to Hedley. I had just settled down for a doze when there was a knock at the door, and I found myself facing a distinctly miffed Hedley. 'Do you mind if I have a look at your bedroom, Mr McDougall?

'No,' I replied, somewhat uncertainly, 'Go ahead.' Having examined my suite, Hedley looked even more miffed, and said, 'Would you like to come and see my room, Mr McDougall?' I was inclined to say, 'Not really', but instead I dutifully followed him to the end of a rather dim corridor, where he let me in to a spartan single room, with an adjoining shower which was not big enough to swing a kitten in, never mind a cat. 'I'm quite sure you won't have any objection to swapping', he stated, rather than asked, and it didn't seem polite to refuse. Hedley chuckled at the luxury that Bill had planned for himself, and I consoled myself with the thought that I probably wouldn't have used the writing room much anyway.

Prior to leaving, Hedley had made arrangements with an Edinburgh outfitter to kit us out with matching suits, but he had omitted to tell me this, and I went in with the impression that I was to choose a suit for myself. 'Could I look at that one?', I asked the outfitter, only to be told that he didn't think it was suitable. The same happened with the next one I looked at, and the next one after that. Finally, the manager said to me, 'Actually sir, you're just here to try on the suit Mr Wright has chosen for you.' He produced a ghastly, silver-coloured affair with lining in the trouser legs. Given that we were to be in Bordeaux in June and that on one day the temperature rose to 120∞F in the exhibition hall, this kit did seem a little out of place. On that particular day bottles of red wine popped their corks, and for a while it was as though the place was under attack with machine-gun fire. It was hard and hot work and it wasn't in Hedley's nature to be a 'frontman' for the company on a trade stand, as he was actually quite shy, and he developed the habit of wandering off for a couple of hours at a time to talk to various acquaintances from the whisky and wine trades, while I was inundated with enquiries and also had to serve free drams of Springbank.

One evening over dinner Hedley told me in confidence that he had invited his nephew, Gordon Wright, to join the company early the following year, with a view to him learning the business and ultimately succeeding Hedley as MD. When I asked how much Gordon already knew about whisky-making, Hedley was forced to admit that he was really a landscape gardener, but that he wanted to settle the succession of the business within the family. Gordon was already a non-executive director of J&A Mitchell & Co Ltd, but he was now to take on an executive position, and, not unnaturally, I wondered how this would affect my role in the company.

Chapter 14
Campbeltown:
Company Cracks

I managed to negotiate a wage increase for the workforce late in 1988, just after the departure of Bill Thomson, when I persuaded Hedley that he ought to improve his staff's pay, which was well below the industry average at the time. I had to approach other distillers who I knew and ask them what sort of rates they were paying their staff in order to have some figures with which to face Hedley. I was forced to do this because Mitchell's had ceased to be members of the SWA and the MDA some years before. Springbank remains the only working distillery in Scotland which is not a member of the SWA. I managed to negotiate a 20-month-long agreement on salaries, and while the packages were pretty basic, excluding pension schemes, company cars and the like, at least remuneration at Springbank was now in line with the rest of the industry.

In 1987, Mr Fraser was dismissed as manager of Cadenhead's shop in Edinburgh, as it was not making any profit. Neil Clapperton took over the retail franchise of Cadenhead's, along with his partner Alan Murray, who had been working in Bell's Broxburn bottling facility. Neil had trained as a window-dresser in the ladies' retail fashion business, and had worked with Richard shops, amongst others.

It came as a very pleasant surprise when at Christmas 1989 several of us received an extra month's salary as a bonus without a word having been said. This was extremely welcome, as I had been instructed by my sister, Grace, that I was to accompany her and her family on a trip to Lucerne in Switzerland for Christmas. When Grace said go, you went; she was that sort of sister. Grace lived in Edinburgh, and could never come to terms with the fact that she had to travel to Glasgow in order to listen to Scottish opera. She found it quite bewildering that the ultimate musical form should be staged in an industrial city in the west rather than in Scotland's capital.

While in Switzerland I met my present wife, Patricia, who was a widow on holiday with her son and daughter-in-law. She had red hair and striking good looks which immediately attracted me. More importantly, perhaps, she had a great sense of humour, and we just liked each other. It was wonderful to have someone to talk to and laugh with again.

Although alcohol was expensive in Switzerland I decided one day that as it was Christmas I would treat myself to a good malt whisky. The barman produced a bottle of Glenfiddich, but I said I would really like something a bit more exotic. He paused, looked behind and below the counter, then offered me the Glenfiddich again. I asked for a double, and warming to the taste I proceeded to have another four during the course of the evening. I didn't feel so warm, however, when the barman presented me with a bill for £50. It was five pounds a shot, and that was in 1989!

In January 1990 Gordon and his wife Vanessa moved to Campbeltown from their home in Ayrshire. When Gordon joined the company I wasn't made aware of whether or not I was expected to train him in the art of whisky-making, or any of the company's other activities. He was 26 years old, and I understood that he was to spend time with a couple of outside companies before joining Springbank full-time. There was a total lack of direction on the part of Hedley as to what Gordon would really do. Gordon himself didn't know what he was supposed to be doing, which made the situation quite tricky for both of us. Hedley was a difficult man to work with in many ways, one of which was the fact that little or no dialogue ever took place between him and his staff, and he would tend to avoid face-to-face confrontation on any issue. His method of dealing with problems was simply to write letters to the members of staff concerned.

Gordon was allotted a space in Hedley's office, which was far from modern in appearance, and featured an extremely elderly roller-shutter desk at which the man himself sat. All of the furniture at Springbank was at least 50 years old, and there was a large open-plan main room with high Victorian desks and regulatory stools. For some reason, I was reminded of Scrooge in *A Christmas Carol*.

Gordon was very friendly, but our relationship was quite difficult, because although I was old enough to be his father, I was aware that he was a company shareholder and an executive director. Policy at Springbank was for everyone to be addressed as 'Mr' or 'Mrs', there were no first-name terms. I was always 'Mr McDougall' to Hedley, and he and Gordon were both 'Mr Wright' to me, which made life quite confusing if nothing else. Gordon had very little to do, and he began to take an interest in the marketing of Springbank. He could express himself well on paper and in person, and he was a very good 'front man' for the organisation. By going through old records he found the names of all the people with whom the company had previously done business, and he proceeded to contact them. In addition to this, Gordon established a close relationship with a number of quite large companies, including Oddbins, at a time when they were really starting to push single malts hard. He also developed overseas sales to a significant extent. In addition to Springbank malt, Gordon sold a variety of other whiskies which we had in stock, potentially for the Cadenhead range, as 'own label' bottlings for chains like Oddbins. Oddbins chose malts from samples presented, and they were bottled quite differently to Cadenhead products, in tall, clear bottles, with cork-mouth finishes, rather than the Cadenhead old-style amber dump or tall green bottles. They did, however, carry the Cadenhead name. This was successful in raising sales, and brought much-needed cash into the company, but this activity was perceived as not being very positive for the Cadenhead image. The other directors of Cadenhead, Hedley and Neil Clapperton, felt that sales to Oddbins detracted from the Cadenhead brand, and because of the quantity Oddbins were buying, they were looking for progressively competitive prices with each deal made. The more whisky sold to Oddbins and subsequently marketed quite cheaply, the harder it became to sell comparable whiskies in the Cadenhead range. Quite a difference of opinion developed between Hedley and Neil on the one hand, and Gordon on the other.

Gordon had made some one-off sales in Korea and Chile, and had developed the Springbank business through the Pol Roger distributors in the UK. He had also found distributors for Springbank in the USA, which turned out to be good business, and opened up the German market to a significant extent. Springbank had long enjoyed a high reputation in Japan, at one time being the leading single malt there, and Gordon made several successful sales trips to the country. It was Gordon who pioneered sales of casks of new Springbank spirit to the general public. This sort of activity has since attracted some very bad publicity, thanks to a number of 'fly by night' opportunists who projected vast returns on whisky, but the Springbank operation was totally above board and offered people a perfectly good deal.

By the June of 1990 my relationship with Pat had flourished to the extent that she came up to Campbeltown from England to live with me. She made a very material difference to my life, and after a few months in the company flat we decided we wanted somewhere of our own. Eventually we bought a newly-built bungalow in the little village of Southend, ten miles south-west of Campbeltown on the way to the Mull of Kintyre itself, overlooking the sea, with views of the coast of Ireland on clear days.

By this time Gordon and I were on first-name terms, and the money that was coming into the company as a result of improved sales made a significant difference to the finances of the business. We were able to upgrade the bottling hall, the mill room and the mash house, along with a dry-goods store in a previously derelict warehouse. Gordon clearly felt that he would be allowed to go on developing the business as he wanted, and he turned his attention to Eaglesome's. This was not actually in his remit, but he, and other members of the family, felt that the shop would benefit from a new approach. It was being run by an old-fashioned grocer called George Cook, who had trained in the Co-operative Society, and had run the local Co-op, which was Campbeltown's only supermarket.

Pat had never been to the west of Scotland before she visited me to stay for the first time in May 1990, and I drove the 140 miles from Campbeltown to meet met her at Glasgow Airport. We were just passing Loch Lomond when she asked, 'Are we nearly there yet?' 'Not exactly,' I replied, 'but another 125 miles or so and we will be.' She thought I was joking, and repeated her question a few miles later as we rounded the head of Loch Long and again by Arrochar and again at Rest and Be Thankful and finally again at Inveraray on Loch Fyne, after which she went quiet. The last three-quarters of an hour of the journey passed in silence; she was obviously wondering what on earth she was letting herself in for.

Next morning she decided to go shopping and was looking forward to going out.

'John, where's the local Sainsbury's?' she asked.

'Glasgow.' I responded, seeing no point in swerving the question.

'Oh…well what about Tesco?'

'No Tesco,' I replied.

'Asda?'

'No Asda'.

Finally I pointed to the Co-op 'superstore', which was about a tenth the size of most supermarkets. 'That's it,' I told her. She looked aghast; I'm sure she didn't believe me and probably spent all day searching the streets for something bigger and better, convinced that this was some sort of practical joke. Despite Campbeltown's retail limitations, Pat agreed to marry me, and the ceremony took place in July 1992 at Ludlow in Shropshire. We produced a special Springbank whisky miniature which we presented to every guest. For Pat, the Campbeltown 'time warp' appeared even more apparent than it had to me, and when we decided to look for a house of our own, she was astonished that there were no estate agents as such, just a few postcard-size photos of properties stuck in the windows of solicitors' offices.

Gordon thought that it would be a good idea if his wife Vanessa and Pat took over the sales administration function of Eaglesome on a job-sharing basis. George Cook was still issuing hand-written invoices for goods which may have been quaint and old-fashioned, but Gordon felt was unacceptable. Lilian Campbell was vehemently opposed to the job-sharing idea, saying that bosses' wives shouldn't be employed by the company in this way.

George Cook was an extremely good shop manager, though he found bar codes and sell-by dates quite difficult to come to terms with. Gordon Wright was determined that the image of Eaglesome's must change, and he wanted it to become a delicatessen-cum-wine and spirits shop. George Cook agreed to retire, and in the spring of 1991 Roger Hanley, from the Exeter Wine Library, was appointed to take over the shop. Gordon took the decision to spend money on re-fitting the premises, and the wines and spirits were presented in a style not dissimilar to that pioneered by Oddbins. I thought it was very effective, but I was beginning to feel unhappy with the way things were being done, as I was, after all, Managing Director of Eaglesome, and all of the changes were being carried out without much consultation. Pat, too, felt fairly left out, as Vanessa Wright and Roger Hanley became great friends, and eventually she left the job-sharing scheme and let the rest get on with it.

In March 1991 I was taken seriously ill and admitted to hospital in Campbeltown, before being transferred by air ambulance to Glasgow. We were in the middle of preparing to move to our new bungalow at the time, so Pat was left with rather a lot on her hands, not to mention the difficulty of getting to visit me in Glasgow. It was only when my sister Grace came from Edinburgh to see me in hospital that I realised I must be *seriously* ill. In fact, the doctors were convinced at first that I had cancer, but ultimately this turned out to be a false alarm. I was in hospital for several weeks, and got home two days before we were due to move. I was barely through the door of our flat, feeling terrible, when Lilian Campbell phoned me with a query about the whisky stocks. Pat left her in no doubt that I was not to be disturbed, and eventually took me away to Hampshire for a while to recuperate, where I could not be involved in Springbank business. I found it hard to forgive Lilian for her insensitivity, although she and Alex had taken the trouble to visit me in the Southern General Hospital. The doctors had told me that I should spend three months resting before returning to work, but inevitably it didn't work out like that.

Hedley, Gordon and Vanessa went to VINEXPO while I was recovering from my time in hospital, and in my absence Denzil was charged with ensuring that everything was packed for the trip. Apparently he forgot to include the hand tools necessary to erect the stand, and my first duty on returning to work was to fire him for negligence on Hedley's instructions. After Denzil's departure, we promoted the stillman Hector Gatt to the role of brewer.

Lilian had decided that her son, Stuart, who had previously worked for Jaeger before becoming a Prudential door-to-door salesman, should be appointed admin manager, with a view to eventually taking over her role. Such an appointment meant that there was a serious danger of the chiefs outnumbering the indians in the organisation. Unfortunately, she sold the idea to Gordon, who then approached me for my opinion. Needless to say, I was far from happy that this had not been discussed with me at a much earlier stage, but eventually Stuart was appointed. Lilian duly retired at the age of 60, after 25 years of service, and was given a retirement party in the White Hart Hotel, at which she was presented with a cask of newly distilled Springbank. The 'outside' workforce had taken a collection and bought her a present. They were far from impressed, therefore, when she turned up for work again the following week, and carried on as if nothing had happened! 'I've got a job here for life,' she used to claim, and as she enjoyed Hedley's backing, she clearly had.

I felt that my opinions and experience no longer carried much weight, and I wondered what the future held for me at Springbank as Gordon's star seemed to be so firmly in the ascendant. I had no idea whether Hedley really approved of Gordon's activities, and to what extent he might take over my function in time. Our respective roles had never been discussed or defined.

With all of this in mind, I began to consider new projects, and in 1992 I became involved in an attempt to buy a distillery. The opportunity arose to purchase Glengarioch distillery at Oldmeldrum in Aberdeenshire, and an all-Scottish consortium was put together to make a bid. It would have been nice to see such a group running an all-Scottish business, and this would have prevented the distillery and its jobs effectively being controlled from overseas, which was what ultimately happened.

We entered into negotiations with Morrison Bowmore Distillers, who owned Glengarioch, and our discussions lasted for several months as we needed a lot of information to enable us to approach institutional investors and venture capitalists. The business plan looked good, but finally the whole deal hinged on a fillings contract between the selling company and the buying company. We raised the asking price of £2.25m, and organised £750,000 of working capital, which was quite an impressive achievement. By late 1992 it looked likely that the project would go ahead, but then Morrison Bowmore announced that they could not fulfil their part of the proposed fillings contract. We re-jigged our figures, and the project was still viable, but by this time, I think, they were keeping their options open, as the Japanese company Suntory, a major shareholder in Morrison Bowmore, looked likely to buy out the whole company, and retain Glengarioch. This was what finally happened, and was a big disappointment to all of us in the consortium. I remain convinced that we could have made a first-class job of establishing and running an excellent, independent business. We were also offering a very good deal for the staff, who were a major consideration in all our deliberations.

One stumbling block in our negotiations concerned the distillery water supply, as there were doubts as to who owned the land where the supply was located, and the formality of the arrangement for its use. Another interesting aspect of Glengarioch was that it had won awards for recycling waste heat, largely due to the efforts of an old trainee friend of mine, Alistair Ross, who had become production director of Morrison Bowmore. They had grown tomatoes and even orchids in hot houses, but this had now become something of a rod for their own back, as due to increased production over the years there was less waste heat available, and a dedicated system for the greenhouses had been installed at additional cost. We had, however, promised to continue running the project for at least a year.

There was some land adjacent to the distillery which could have been developed for housing, a project would have helped us recoup some of our purchase price. I suspect that following one set of discussions we had with Morrison Bowmore, they realised the potential value of this area of land, and that helped their decision not to sell. Despite its failure, the exercise had been a very stimulating one in which to be involved.

Meanwhile, in the summer of 1993 Hedley appointed me as a director of the company. This followed Neil Clapperton's promotion to the post of chief executive director of William Cadenhead, and was done while Gordon was on business in Scandinavia. With Neil's appointment, Gordon's power over Cadenhead was seriously diminished. At the time he appointed me a director, Hedley asked whether I would be staying at Springbank until I retired, as that was what the company wanted. At that stage I was able to reply honestly that I would like to, as I felt I had one of the best jobs in the business, despite my misgivings about the 'politics' of the organisation.

Gordon and I had been working on re-packaging the Cadenhead range of whiskies, replacing the old amber dump bottles with their black labels with tall, green bottles with cork finishes, and a screen-printing effect of the name Cadenhead and other details on the actual bottle, with a space to fit in the printed label. The Cadenhead re-design became Neil's project, but I think it was forgotten that Gordon and I had actually done all the work. Neil now also began to be heavily involved in the presentation and packaging of Springbank as well as Cadenhead whiskies, which reduced Gordon's role in that area too. It was made clear to Gordon that in all matters relating to Cadenhead, Neil was the boss. An Edinburgh designer, George Redpath, was involved by Neil in the re-design, and it soon became apparent that Neil wanted him to become more closely involved in the work of the company in general. Previously I had been doing all the specifying and purchasing of bottling materials, but now I was expected to have everything relating to that side of the operation okayed by George Redpath.

In 1993, Gordon decided that the company should get back into the retail drinks trade, not with a bar, but with a wine bar-cum-seafood restaurant. This was to be developed in disused storerooms at the rear of the Eaglesome shop, where there was also a courtyard. The idea seemed sound, and must have had Hedley's approval. The wine bar duly opened just before Christmas 1993, and it looked splendid. Gordon saw the wine bar as a way of selling some of the extensive range of wine carried by Eaglesome. Some of the money generated by Gordon's sales was ploughed into the new wine bar, which he felt would be a great place to offer wine and whisky tastings and could also be used for company entertaining. The concept was excellent, but unfortunately the location was wrong. There were not enough people visiting Campbeltown during the summer to carry the business through the long winter months. Matters within Eaglesome were complicated when Roger Hanley resigned, following a row with Vanessa Wright, and a rapid succession of managers followed. It soon became apparent that the wine bar was not going to be a success, and Hedley insisted late in 1995 that it should be closed down. A revamp of Eaglesome ensued, and the wine bar area became an office for Cadenhead, which meant that we saw rather more of Neil Clapperton than had previously been the case. Vanessa Wright then left Eaglesome.

Chapter 15
Campbeltown:
Conclusions and Kelso

In August 1994 Roy Allan died. I had always liked Roy, who was from a highly respected distilling family. He had two brothers who were distillers, and had been brought up at Dalwhinnie Distillery in Inverness-shire, where his father was manager. His brother, Ted, was manager of Linkwood Distillery at Elgin, and later manager of the new Inver House Distillers' plant at Airdrie in the sixties. Brother Jimmy ran Benrinnes Distillery, near Aberlour. When Roy died, an era at Springbank came to an end, and Hedley had long looked on him as something of a father figure, finally making him a director of Mitchell's after his retirement.

Roy had been at Springbank for more than 40 years, so there was a great turnout for his funeral. Among the mourners was Frank McHardy, who had been Roy's assistant manager, and, briefly, manager before I went there. He had left Springbank to join the management team at Bushmills Distillery on the Antrim coast of Northern Ireland, but had always kept in touch with events at Springbank, especially via Lilian Campbell. Following Roy's death there were two vacant directorships, one in Cadenhead and one in Eaglesome, and Lilian Campbell was appointed to the boards of both, while Gordon was removed from the board of Cadenhead.

Gordon Wright was friendly with Mark Reynier, of Mark Reynier Fine Wines in London, as we had done some specialist bottling for him in the past. On one occasion he asked us to bottle some Macallan which he owned. It was in American barrels, rather than ex-sherry butts, so the whisky was not the usual style for which Macallan is renowned. Somehow Alan Shiach, chairman of Macallan Distillers at that time, and a Hollywood scriptwriter to boot, heard about this, and proceeded to write to Hedley, complaining bitterly about his audacity at getting involved in bottling Macallan which was not representative of the whisky which was being marketed by the company itself. Hedley stuck to his guns, as did Mark Reynier, as neither had done anything wrong, and the whisky was duly bottled and sold. I got to nose and taste it, and I thought it was absolutely delicious, being 'exposed' rather than masked by sherry. In my opinion it was very much a 'stand alone' dram, and a real credit to the name of Macallan.

The company has a record of bottling whisky from other distilleries going back about 170 years, and they had always given the provenance of these bottlings without asking permission from the distillers. Some distillers take exception to this, most notably William Grant & Sons, J&G Grant of Glenfarclas, and Laphroaig. Hedley had been in and out of court with them several times over the years.

By 1994 Pat and I had decided that we would like to stay in Campbeltown for the foreseeable future, partly because she had got a good job with the RAF as the housing officer at Machrihanish. Although the base was being wound down, it was still a busy place at the time. I felt that despite the problems at Springbank I wanted to stay on and continue my work there. We decided to build a new house above Campbeltown Loch, looking across to Ben Gullion. This seemed an appropriate place for a distiller to live, bearing in mind the words of the song made famous all over the world by Andy Stewart: 'Campbeltown Loch I wish you were whisky/Campbeltown Loch,

och aye./Campbeltown Loch I wish you were whisky/then I could drink ye dry.'

We moved into the new house in March 1995. It was a split-level property with brilliant views, and we hoped to live there at least until my retirement. The site of the house was actually very close to where my ill-fated caravan had been anchored a few years before, and I just hoped that this would be a warmer and more secure place in winter.

Gordon had long had kidney problems, and it came to the point in 1995 where he had to have a home dialysis kit. He made light of this, but it meant that when he went abroad on sales trips he had to arrange in advance for the necessary equipment to be available in each town or city where he stayed, so that the process of dialysis could take place overnight. The man went up by leaps and bounds in my estimation for the way he handled what must have been at the very least a tiresome and difficult situation.

In 1995 a new company called Springbank Distillers Ltd was set up to take over UK distribution from Eaglesome. This made sense because it gave the distributor greater identity with the brand, and a property was acquired on Longrow to house the new company. A young man by the name of Ewan Mitchell was employed as its salesman, which effectively meant that Gordon no longer had any say over sales of Springbank in Britain.

Back in 1992 I had began trading some of the stocks of whisky I had built up through a company called Lifton House which I had set up in 1989. Hedley steadfastly refused to consider any sort of company pension fund for his staff, and I saw this as a way of providing for my retirement. I bought new fillings as well as selling some of my existing casks to outsiders. The company was well aware of what I was doing, and considering their lack of interest in pension provisions for their employees, it wasn't unreasonable that I should do something to prevent me starving in the years ahead. Along with a property developer friend of mine, Jim Macmorran, I also formed a company called Aberdeen Distillers Ltd, purely as an investment vehicle and a mechanism for buying and selling whisky stocks.

In October 1995 Jim Macmorran was conducting some business with Neil Clapperton on behalf of Aberdeen Distillers Ltd, and late one afternoon I got a phonecall from Hedley at 4.55pm. 'Mr McDougall,' he said, 'I wish you to come to the secretary's office at ten o'clock in the morning to discuss my nephew, and also your involvement with the firm Aberdeen Distillers Ltd.' Then he put the phone down before I had a chance to reply.

When I turned up at the office next day Hedley was behind the company secretary's desk, looking like a Victorian schoolmaster. All that was missing was the black gown and mortar board. The company secretary, John McTaggart, was sitting on his right. Hedley commenced: 'It has come to my attention that you have an involvement with Aberdeen Distillers, indeed, you are a director of the company. Do you not consider this to be a conflict of interests?' I pointed out that I had already told Hedley of my involvement, and that most people in his company were aware of my out of hours activities, but Jim Macmorran had managed to upset Neil Clapperton, and clearly his response had been to complain to Hedley. It was suggested that I should resign my directorship of Aberdeen Distillers, which I duly did, as it didn't affect my investment in the company, and was no problem for Jim. I was then queried about Gordon's performance.

●   ●   ●

During 1995 we set up a secondary bottling hall in a previously derelict building, which gave us the opportunity to bottle rum, gin and vodka for the Cadenhead range. Neil Clapperton came up with the idea of marketing something which he wanted to call 'Triple S' - Springbank Single Spirit. This was new spirit, and he had the idea that some of the trendy bars in and around cities could do well with it. I never did get to know whether it was successful, but at the very least it was another packaging exercise which kept people employed. By this time, Cadenhead not only had its Edinburgh shop, but also one in London's Covent Garden. Neil had plans to open a chain of franchised Cadenhead shops all over Europe, which was interesting in theory, but would probably have been a disaster if it had ever happened.

Early in 1996 Gordon and I took legal advice, and eventually we decided we would stay and see what happened. It was, however, a time of great uncertainty and unease. I loved the whole business of making whisky, and was very proud to be running the most authentic family-run concern in the industry, where everything from the buying of the barley to the bottling and worldwide distribution of the finished product was controlled from Campbeltown. I felt a great deal of distress and disappointment with the way things had worked out.

We requested a meeting with Hedley on the May Day holiday to try to clear the air, and he told us that he would meet us at 5pm the following Wednesday. On Tuesday Gordon was in hospital in Glasgow for a routine check-up, and by coincidence a kidney became available for transplant while he was there, and he stayed in hospital to have the operation. The meeting was, therefore, postponed. We had planned to speak to Hedley about the operating conditions for us at Springbank, having consulted with our lawyers about the tack we should take.

A fortnight after the projected meeting, while Gordon was still in hospital, I received a letter from Hedley inviting me to explain why I was still a shareholder in Aberdeen Distillers Ltd. The letter also said that information had been received to the effect that I was putting business in the way of that company, which meant a conflict of interest. This was untrue.

My lawyer insisted that under no circumstances should I attend the meeting with Hedley, and he told me that he would write to him saying that I would only attend a meeting at which he could be present. I therefore didn't meet Hedley, and later the same afternoon I received a letter from the company lawyer, informing me that I was suspended on full pay pending an enquiry into my activities with Aberdeen Distillers Ltd, unless I chose to meet Hedley as previously arranged. I replied to the effect that I didn't think I had any case to answer, but that I would be happy to attend a meeting with my lawyer present. Another letter arrived from the company lawyer the following day, saying that I had one final chance to meet Hedley and rebut the allegations made against me. I was given three days in which to agree to this. That obviously left no time for my lawyer to take statements from people involved, and so we refused.

I saw Gordon in hospital, when he was recuperating from his kidney operation. He had received a letter from Hedley informing him about my situation, but saying that there was nothing for him to worry about; everything was under control, and that he should just get well. Gordon and I agreed to call an EGM of the company, at which we would have had a majority, and been able to outflank Hedley and his supporters. Unfortunately, Gordon suffered a relapse, and was not fit enough to travel to Campbeltown for the meeting, which had to be called off. This gave our opposition the vital time they needed to regroup, and Hedley proceeded to serve interim interdicts on Gordon and I, banning us from being directors of the company.

While he was still recuperating, Gordon received a letter from the company, telling him that Springbank Distillers Ltd was going to take on worldwide distribution of Springbank whisky, and as Gordon was not employed by that company, he was therefore being made redundant. Furthermore, having taken out the interim interdict against Gordon and I, Hedley employed a security firm, complete with a uniformed guard on the gate, in order to prevent 'undesirables' from entering the Springbank premises.

We called another EGM, and when Gordon, his mother and I turned up at the gate for the meeting Hedley welcomed Gordon and his mother, but refused to let me enter. He proceeded to hand over another of his letters, this time informing me that I had effectively dismissed myself by leaving my post without permission. This was, of course, disputed. I contended that I was constructively dismissed.

A period of bitter litigation ensued, with Gordon and his family and myself fighting to get the interdicts lifted. Eventually, I decided that this was no longer my fight, and I bowed out. I began to work full-time as a broker with my Lifton House company; in 1996 the brokerage market was quite active, so I was kept busy buying and selling casks of whisky.

Gordon had been preparing his exit, and teamed up with Mark Reynier and Simon Coughlin in an independent bottling company of their own called Murray McDavid. Here Gordon was able to use the many contacts he had made worldwide in the whisky business, and Murray McDavid went head-to-head with Cadenhead.

As a broker, much of my stock consisted of casks of Springbank which I had previously bought as new make, and there had never been a problem in selling these when I was with the company. Indeed, as late as the summer of 1995 they had bought from me a quantity of Highland Park, and had never had a problem with my hobby. Now, however, when I began to try to sell my Springbank, they refused to process legitimate delivery orders. This effectively removed my ability to make a living. One day a Sheriff's Officer turned up at our house with an inhibition order preventing me from selling any of our properties, as J&A Mitchell were effectively suing me for £20,000. I found the whole matter very puzzling, as £20,000 was the amount of money I had paid to Mitchell's via Lifton House. The case was due to be heard in the Court of Session in Edinburgh, but at the last moment Hedley's lawyers announced that he had decided to drop the action. By this time I had spent several thousands of pounds on legal fees, and had suffered considerable stress. At the preliminary hearing the Judge had intimated to Hedley's lawyers that unless they could produce significant new information then I had no case to answer, which was probably why he decided to proceed no further. Needless to say, Hedley did not attend the preliminary hearing in person.

The inhibitions were duly lifted, and Gordon and I now decided to go to an industrial tribunal with our cases for unfair dismissal. The day before the hearing, Hedley conceded defeat, and Gordon was granted the maximum sum available in respect of lost earnings. I couldn't prove a loss of income, unfortunately, so I got the minimum amount, which barely covered my legal fees.

In order to get Hedley to process orders for the Springbank whisky I owned, we had to set up a new company in Pat's name, called PJ Trading, so that she, rather than I, owned the whisky. I received dozens of calls of support from all over the world, offering good wishes now that I was no longer with Springbank. Much though these were appreciated, good wishes didn't pay bills, and I had to begin brokering with a vengeance. By late 1996 it was becoming obvious that financial problems were looming in the Far East. I seem to remember that on the day that Chris Patten left Hong Kong as the last British Governor, Thailand announced that it was bankrupt. This, inevitably, had a domino effect through Far Eastern economies, including Japan and Korea, where important whisky markets had been developed in recent years. This led to very difficult trading conditions within the whisky industry, and I probably couldn't have chosen a worse time to branch out on my own as a stockholder and whisky trader, but I had no option. In any case, whisky has always been a cyclical business, with times of boom and bust, so we just carried on trading.

In October 1996 I relinquished all interests in Aberdeen Distillers Ltd, and allowed Jim Macmorran a free hand to get on with his business. I established with my cousin Rob Bateman a company called Roxburgh Holdings, based in Rob's home town of Kelso in the Borders, which was to hold stocks of malt whiskies to feed back into Lifton House for future sales. As the financial situations in the Far East was making sales of casks difficult, we decided to bottle some of our stocks and offer it to the general public. We launched a new brand by the name of Calchou, which would market single malts from our own stocks. Calchou is the ancient name for Kelso, and it was given to the monks of Selkirk by King David I in 1128 when they settled in Kelso. Calchou means 'chalk ridge', with scholarly opinion divided as to whether the name is Anglo-Saxon or Gaelic in origin.

Trying to establish a new brand is always difficult, and in our first full year of trading with Calchou, the high value of the pound kept many overseas visitors away from Britain, and the terrible weather during the summer did nothing to help either. We were, however, heartened by the sales of Calchou, and the interest shown in it. We established it on all the best shelves in the Borders and beyond, and export sales were made to Germany and Japan.

The Borders had enjoyed a proud distilling heritage in days gone by, with Kelso having its own distillery, and as recently as 1824 there was a distiller by the name of Mason resident in the town's Horsemarket. There were also two distilleries near Langholm, and one in Hawick. By establishing our new venture in Kelso we were, in a modest way, continuing the whisky heritage of the area. The whisky industry sets great store by 'heritage', as it is a vital tool in selling the product.

The real heritage in the whisky business is not so much about places but more to do with people. Everyone who works in the business, past or present, is part of the real heritage of whisky-making. When you pick up a bottle of Scotch it isn't just filled with whisky…it also represents the area where it was made and the people who made it.

I have been extremely fortunate in knowing some fascinating characters during my career in the Scotch whisky industry to date. Here's to everyone who has made my working life so interesting and so rewarding. I wouldn't have changed it for anything.

Glossary

bourbon	Whisky produced in the USA from a mash with a minimum 51 percent corn content. Bourbon casks are charred before use, which imparts a distinctive flavour to the spirit.
bushel	The dry measure of eight Imperial gallons. Regarded by the SWA as equal to 25.4kg.
Coffey still	Also known as a *column still* or *patent still*, this is an apparatus for distilling whisky from grain. It consists of two columns – the analyser and the rectifier, and takes its name from Aeneas Coffey, one time Inspector-General of Excise in Ireland. Distillation in the *Coffey still* is continuous, which makes for faster distillation of larger quantities of spirit than is possible using a copper pot still.
column still	see *Coffey still*.
condenser	Attached to the neck of the still, the *condenser* consists of a system of water-cooled tubes which reduce the vapour from the still into liquid alcohol.
clearic	New, unmatured spirit, clear in colour.
dark grains	A cattle feed, made from a mixture of *draff* and pot ale.
draff	Spent grist left in the mashtun after mashing.
dreg	Colloquial name for the residual leftovers from distillation – formerly bought by farmers and used as fertiliser.
dried grains	Cattle feed made from spent mashed cereal.
feints	The impure spirit which flows after the 'middle cut' of the *low wines* has been collected during distillation.
fractionation	Separation by distillation into component parts.
hogshead	A size of oak cask commonly used in the whisky industry. It has a capacity of approx. 55 gallons, or 250 litres.
Ileach	A native of the Hebridean island of Islay.
'Joe'	Colloquial name for wash taken illegally from the washback to drink.
low wines	The product of the first distillation in the *wash still*.
lyne arm	The pipe which connects the top of the still with the *condenser*

mashtun	The vessel in which grist is mixed with hot water to dissolve fermentable sugars.
patent still	see *Coffey still*.
pot ale	The liquor left in the *low wines* or *wash still after* the initial distillation.
rye whiskey	Whisky produced from a mash with a minimum 51 percent rye grain content.
silent season	The period of the year when a distillery is *silent* or unproductive. This period is usually during the summer months, when distillers were traditionally forced to stop making whisky due to lack of water.
sour-mash whiskey	Sour Mash whiskey is *bourbon* or Tennesse whiskey in which part of the previous day's mash is used to start the fermentation of the next batch. Thus, all the mash is 'related'. The process is considered to reinforce the flavour and bouquet of the whiskey.
spent grains	See *draff*.
spent wash	See *pot ale*.
spirit still	The second still in which malt whisky distillation takes place, also known as the *low wines still*.
steam coil	Steam heating of stills superseded coal-firing from the 1880s onwards, becoming particularly popular in the 1960s. A metal *steam coil* is the preferred method of heating *spirit stills*.
steam kettle	While the *steam coil* is favoured in *spirit stills*, thin-walled cylinders, known as *kettles*, are usually fitted to *wash stills*.
surfactant	A substance which reduces surface tension and thus foaming and frothing.
swan neck	The neck of the still, below the *lyne arm*.
tun	Usually refers to a *mashtun*, though rather confusingly, the *mashtuns* in a distillery are located in the mash house, while the *washbacks* are situated in the tun room.
wash still	The first still in which malt whisky distillation takes place.
washback	The vessel in which *wort* is fermented.
worm	A forerunner of the *condenser*. A coiled copper pipe set in a *worm tub* filled with cold water. In the *worm* the vapour from the still condenses into liquid alcohol.
wort	The liquid produced in the mashing process. Broadly speaking, *wort* is a solution of fermentable sugars.
yield	The amount of alcohol produced from a given quantity of malted barley.

212

Index

(Distillery and product names in italics)

Thank you for using your library